Israel: God's Glory

Breaking the Bread of Revelation
Volume 3

Brian McCallum

Israel: God's Glory

Breaking the Bread of Revelation

Volume 3

Faith Library Publications®

Unless otherwise indicated, all scripture quotations are taken from the *King James Version* of the Bible. Public domain.

28 27 26 27 25 24 23 07 06 05 04 03 02 01

Breaking the Bread of Revelation, Volume 3—
Israel: God's Glory
ISBN-13: 978-0-89276-934-6
ISBN-10: 0-89276-934-3

First edition 1990. Faith Library Publications edition 2023.
Printed in the USA

In the U.S. write:
Kenneth Hagin Ministries
P.O. Box 50126
Tulsa, OK 74150-0126
1-888-28-FAITH
rhema.org

In Canada write:
Kenneth Hagin Ministries of Canada
P.O. Box 335, Station D
Etobicoke (Toronto), Ontario
Canada M9A 4X3
1-866-70-RHEMA
rhemacanada.org

Contents

Author's Preface

This book is the third in a series of exposition and commentary on the Book of Revelation, entitled "Breaking the Bread of Revelation."

The first in this series, *Breaking the Bread of Revelation,* discussed chapters 1 through 6 of the last book in our Bible. In this first volume, we saw that the Revelation of Jesus Christ was given to the Church to communicate grace and peace concerning the present time and the future.

Having received that, God's people are free to be fully involved in the work of the Church today of preaching the Gospel to all nations, being used by the Spirit of God to take a people for His Name out of them.

In our study of chapter 6 of Revelation, we looked into the first six seals being opened. We saw that the sixth seal revealed a time of overcoming on the part of the Church and a great harvest being gathered in while the Lord poured out the former and the latter rain on all flesh. In volume 1, chapter 9, we also had a first look at the part the modern nation of Israel will play in gathering this great harvest of souls for the Father God.

Here, in Volume 3, we will look at what the Word says further on that subject, both in Revelation chapter 7 and onward, and in associated Old and New Testament prophecies.

We will see believing Israelites (washed in the blood of Jesus Christ) gleaning in the harvest fields that the Church has already harvested.

As in Jesus' day and the Church's day, we will see great opposition from Satan and his operatives. But, most importantly, we will see God conclude in His master performance all things that the prophets have said will come to pass.

Then the heaven of heavens will release Jesus Christ to return to earth to rule and reign here with His saints. What glory that will be!

I strongly recommend that if you have not already done so, you read *Breaking the Bread of Revelation, Volume 1* and *Seven Letters to Seven Churches, Volume 2* of this series, which deals with Jesus Christ's personal admonition to His Body the Church for the time in which we are living.

May the Spirit of Truth help, bless, and guide you as you apply yourselves to the study of God's Word.

Brian McCallum
Tulsa, Oklahoma
June 1990

Chapter 1

God's Mercy in Israel

Revelation chapter 7 marks an interlude—a time of mercy—between the Rapture of the Gentile Church and the Great Tribulation. Although the Church will be caught away from the earth, God will still have His testimony on the earth. However, it will be a limited testimony compared with what has happened in the time of the Gentile Church.

I would liken the Church Age harvest and Israel's part in it to Israel's natural harvest and the gleanings of that harvest. In the Word, God repeatedly likens our work of preaching the Gospel to that harvest.

When you harvest, you cut the main part of the fields. However, rocks, corners, and other places in your fields may remain unharvested. And as we saw in the biblical story of Boaz and Ruth, some parts of a field may be left unharvested on purpose. If this is so spiritually speaking, God will raise up someone to go after those gleanings that remain.

The Four Corners of the Earth

REVELATION 7:1–4

1 And after these things I saw four angels standing on the four corners of the earth, holding the four winds of the earth, that the wind should not blow on the earth, nor on the sea, nor on any tree.

2 And I saw another angel ascending from the east, having the seal of the living God: and he cried with a loud voice to the four angels, to whom it was given to hurt the earth and the sea,
3 Saying, Hurt not the earth, neither the sea, nor the trees, till we have sealed the servants of our God in their foreheads.
4 And I heard the number of them which were sealed: and there were sealed an hundred and forty and four thousand of all the tribes of the children of Israel.

Here's what God said He will do during the period immediately following the Rapture. The people who remain on the earth in Israel will be convinced by the events that have happened up to and including the Rapture that Jesus is their Messiah.

God will seal 12,000 Jews out of each of the 12 tribes of Israel to do the gleaning of the Church's harvest fields. These Jewish believers will evangelize their nation and the world in the time that remains, or the time generally referred to as the Tribulation.

John uses symbolic words in Revelation chapter 7. For example, we know he's referring to Israel, because he mentions all 12 tribes. Another way we know is by John's use of the word "earth."

What 'Earth' Symbolizes

John saw four angels *"standing on the four corners of the earth"* (Rev. 7:1). The word "earth" can mean just what it says—this planet we live on or the soil we plant things in. "Earth" can also symbolically mean Israel. Let's see how.

Jesus wept over Jerusalem because He came to the nation of Israel and showed God's will to the Jews. But they rejected Him and His message. As He wept, He said, "You've rejected God's prophets repeatedly throughout your history."

The prophet Jeremiah wept over Jerusalem long before Jesus did. According to Jeremiah 22:1 he prophesied, "*Thus saith the Lord; Go down to the house of the king of Judah.*" Who is Judah? That's the southern kingdom, or the southern half of Israel.

The prophecy continues, "*Speak there this word, and say, Hear the word of the Lord, O king of Judah, that sittest upon the throne of David* [David was king over all Israel], *thou, and thy servants, and thy people that enter in by these gates*" (Jer. 22:1–2). It is evident that Jeremiah is talking to Israel—God's heritage and His covenant people.

Then Jeremiah prophesies in the 29th verse, "*O earth, earth, earth, hear the word of the Lord.*" Who is he addressing—the whole world? No, he is addressing *the nation of Israel* and warning them of the judgment that would come and the effects of the disobedience of their kings. He closes the prophecy with this statement.

JEREMIAH 22:30

30 Thus saith the Lord, Write ye this man childless, a man that shall not prosper in his days: for no man of his seed shall prosper, sitting upon the throne of David, and ruling any more in Judah.

This is a reference to Jehoiachin, a king who was disobedient. God cut him off, not only because of his own disobedience but also his father's before him. The prophet Jeremiah is referring to Israel when he speaks to the "earth" in verse 29.

Is this the only place where he does such a thing? No.

JEREMIAH 25:1

1 The word that came to Jeremiah concerning all the people of Judah in the fourth year of Jehoiakim the son of Josiah king of Judah, that was in the first year of Nebuchadrezzar king of Babylon.

He's prophesying to Israel again. He said,

JEREMIAH 25:29

29 For, lo, I begin to bring evil on the city which is called by my name, and should ye be utterly unpunished? Ye shall not be unpunished: for I will call for a sword upon all the inhabitants of the earth, saith the Lord of hosts.

Who is God bringing judgment against—the whole world? No, against that nation He called *"the inhabitants of the earth."* Again, "earth" symbolizes Israel.

In the first chapter of Micah, we hear the word of the Lord to Hezekiah and different kings of Judah concerning Samaria and Jerusalem (both the northern and southern kingdoms).

MICAH 1:2–5

2 Hear, all ye people; hearken, O earth, and all that therein is: and let the Lord God be witness against you, the Lord from his holy temple.

3 For, behold, the Lord cometh forth out of his place, and will come down, and tread upon the high places of the earth.

4 And the mountains shall be molten under him, and the valleys shall be cleft, as wax before the fire, and as the waters that are poured down a steep place.

5 For the transgression of Jacob is all this, and for the sins of the house of Israel. What is the transgression of Jacob? is it not Samaria? and what are the high places of Judah? are they not Jerusalem?

God is talking about judging Israel, His own people, for judgment begins at the house of the Lord (1 Peter 4:17). Because God's people have sinned and disobeyed Him, He must judge them to bring forth righteousness on the earth.

So God is referring to Israel when His prophet says, *"Hear, all ye people; hearken, O earth, and all that therein is."* He's not talking to the whole world. He's talking to *Israel*—about them, about their lives, and how He must judge them.

Examples From Revelation

In Revelation 16:14 we see another reference about the earth. *"For they are the spirits of devils* [spirits that come forth], *working miracles, which go forth unto the kings of the earth and of the whole world."* That's Israel first of all. Earth here does not refer to the whole world or He would not have said *" 'and' of the whole world."*

Returning to the 13th chapter of Revelation, John says, *"And I stood upon the sand of the sea, and saw a beast rise up out of the sea, having seven heads and ten horns. . . . And I beheld another beast coming up out of the earth"* (Rev. 13:1, 11).

The first beast is the Antichrist. He comes up out of *the sea.* (We'll soon see what the sea symbolizes.)

The second beast in Revelation 13 comes up out of *the earth*—out of Israel. He is the False Prophet. (We will study more about these two beasts in a later chapter of this book.)

Chapter 2

✡

Strife Restrained

Return with me to our text, Revelation 7:1, *"After these things I saw four angels standing on the four comers of the earth* [the planet], *holding the four winds of the earth, that the wind should not blow on the earth."* Let's examine the use of the word "winds" and the phrase "winds of the earth."

The earth, being a globe, doesn't have "corners," so we can be sure our text is talking about the whole earth—from all four points of the compass or from all directions. "Earth" means the globe we live on. "Winds" represent strife. Therefore, the phrase *"holding the four winds of the earth"* means restraining the strife that is seeking to come.

The following two scriptures further illustrate this.

DANIEL 7:2

2 Daniel spake and said, I saw in my vision by night, and, behold, the four winds of the heaven strove upon the great sea.

JEREMIAH 49:34–38

34 The word of the Lord that came to Jeremiah the prophet against Elam in the beginning of the reign of Zedekiah king of Judah, saying,

35 Thus saith the Lord of hosts; Behold, I will break the bow of Elam, the chief of their might.

36 And upon Elam will I bring the four winds from the four quarters of heaven, and will scatter them toward all those winds; and

there shall be no nation whither the outcasts of Elam shall not come.
37 For I will cause Elam to be dismayed before their enemies, and before them that seek their life: and I will bring evil upon them, even my fierce anger, saith the Lord; and I will send the sword after them, till I have consumed them:
38 And I will set my throne in Elam, and will destroy from thence the king and the princes, saith the Lord.

Most of us are aware that the potential for strife is very great in the Middle East. Every time you hear or see news reports from that part of the world, some kind of strife is surfacing. Nevertheless, strife in the Middle East has never reached anywhere near the potential of what it could.

Jesus said in Matthew chapter 24 there would be wars in the end times, and there are—but the Middle East isn't experiencing the conflict it could be. That's because it's being held back. God said it's being held back by the four angels.

However, a great deal of hate is being manifested between the peoples of the Middle East. Hate is a force like love is a force, except it's a negative force, and it commissions the wrong kind of spirits. Love gives God a way to act on the earth. But if hate is in manifestation, you will see the fruit of hate unless something stops it.

The Unseen Work of Angels

What is that "something"? The Spirit of God is saying in our text that four angels are holding back the strife that seeks to envelop that part of the world. And they will continue to do this until God's purposes have been fulfilled in the Middle East.

God said the winds of the earth should not blow on the earth, on the sea, or on any tree. Is this Bible a book about the redemption of soil, water, and wood? Or is it a book about the redemption of mankind? The answer, of course, is mankind. What God is saying must apply to man. The proof of this is found in Revelation chapter 7.

REVELATION 7:2–3
2 And I saw another angel ascending from the east, having the seal of the living God: and he cried with a loud voice to the four angels, to whom it was given to hurt the earth and the sea,
3 Saying, Hurt not the earth, neither the sea, nor the trees, till we have sealed the servants of our God in their foreheads.

In other words, something of spiritual significance is going to happen in the Middle East before a general war or some other conflict envelops that whole area and costs many human lives.

Israel: Past and Present

God said, "Don't hurt the earth. Don't hurt the sea. Don't hurt the trees until we have sealed the servants of God on their foreheads." We saw that "earth" represented Israel. Soon we will see what the sea represents.

But first you may ask, "Why is all this attention focused on Israel, anyway?" God put it there, so why argue about it? He wants us to see many things from His dealings with that one nation.

One thing He wants us to learn is how *sure* His Word is—how absolutely sure that when God has said something out of His mouth, it *will* come to pass. It won't make a difference if it takes 10,000 years. It will still come to pass just the way He said it.

In the Garden of Eden, God promised He would send a Savior, didn't He? It was approximately 4,000 years later that Jesus came. During that time, people no doubt remembered God's promise and wondered, "Well, He must not have meant it." People say the same thing today. It's a serious mistake to doubt God's Word.

God means everything He says just like He says it, and it will all come to pass, because He sees to it that it does.

And He wants us to see from His dealings with the nation of Israel what He plans and wills to do with *every* nation. God has no favorite nation. He loves all men the same way. God doesn't love one more than another. He has the same care for all.

Today we are living in an age where His care for mankind can be manifested to all if we, the Church, the Body of Christ, will be obedient and be the means through which God can manifest His power and love.

Again, this is why there is so much attention in the Word of God on that one nation, Israel. God wants us to see His complete dealings with her, from start to finish, and to know that what He says is absolutely so.

From the scriptures we have studied so far, we see Israel will have an important and essential part in the end-time harvest that we, the Church, are already involved in. These scriptures are showing us some details about this great, worldwide harvest and its final stage.

Chapter 3

By the Sea

REVELATION 7:3–4

3 . . . Hurt not the earth, neither the sea, nor the trees, till we have sealed the servants of our God in their foreheads.

4 And I heard the number of them which were sealed: and there were sealed an hundred and forty and four thousand of all the tribes of the children of Israel.

The word "sea" is used symbolically, so let's see what it refers to. We will find an answer in Jeremiah chapter 49.

Here, the Spirit of God is prophesying through Jeremiah concerning different nations in the Middle East—that is, nations around the eastern Mediterranean. This prophecy refers to their future.

God says a great deal about Israel and the nations surrounding her in the Bible. He doesn't say something about *every* nation in the world, but what He says is enough for us to understand and do His will.

A Word to Syria

For example, Damascus, one of the oldest continuously occupied cities in the world, is mentioned in this passage. It is, and always has been, the capital of Syria. The prophet says,

JEREMIAH 49:23–27

23 Concerning Damascus [Syria or Damascus]. Hamath is confounded, and Arpad: for they have heard evil tidings: they are fainthearted; there is sorrow on the sea; it cannot be quiet.

24 Damascus is waxed feeble, and turneth herself to flee, and fear hath seized on her: anguish and sorrows have taken her, as a woman in travail.
25 How is the city of praise not left, the city of my joy!
26 Therefore her young men shall fall in her streets, and all the men of war shall be cut off in that day, saith the Lord of hosts.
27 And I will kindle a fire in the wall of Damascus, and it shall consume the palaces of Benhadad.

The prophet is predicting something will come in the future. He says turmoil or upheaval in the sea cannot be quiet. He relates Syria to *the sea.*

Later, in Jeremiah chapter 51, he prophesies about Babylon.

JEREMIAH 51:35–40, 42–43

35 The violence done to me and to my flesh be upon Babylon, shall the inhabitant of Zion say; and my blood upon the inhabitants of Chaldea, shall Jerusalem say.
36 Therefore thus saith the Lord; Behold, I will plead thy cause, and take vengeance for thee; and I will dry up her sea, and make her springs dry.
37 And Babylon shall become heaps, a dwellingplace for dragons, and astonishment, and an hissing, without an inhabitant.
38 They shall roar together like lions: they shall yell as lions' whelps.
39 In their heat I will make their feasts, and I will make them drunken, that they may rejoice, and sleep a perpetual sleep, and not wake, saith the Lord.
40 I will bring them down like lambs to the slaughter, like rams with he goats.

Then, in verses 42 and 43, the prophet says *the sea* has come up upon Babylon.

42 The sea is come up upon Babylon: she is covered with the multitude of the waves thereof.

43 Her cities are a desolation, a dry land, and a wilderness, a land wherein no man dwelleth, neither doth any son of man pass thereby.

Did the ocean ever flow over the kingdom of Babylon? No, it never did. What *did* come up over Babylon? The Medes and the Persians came in one night and seized the kingdom from King Belshazzar, who saw the handwriting on the wall. (See Daniel chapter 5.) That was the very night he lost his kingdom and his life. *The sea* did come upon Babylon.

It should be noted that modern Iraq, part of Iran (formerly Persia), and some of modern Syria comprise the ancient Babylonian Kingdom.

Words for More Nations

Quite a few nations are involved in the following passage.

ZECHARIAH 10:10–11

10 I will bring them again also out of the land of Egypt, and gather them out of Assyria; and I will bring them into the land of Gilead and Lebanon; and place shall not be found for them.

The Assyrian Kingdom is modern Iraq, for the most part. And the Assyrian Kingdom possessed the land before Babylon did.

11 And he [God performing His Word] shall pass through the sea with affliction, and shall smite the waves in the sea, and all the deeps of the river shall dry up: and the pride of Assyria shall be brought down, and the sceptre of Egypt shall depart away.

In other words, God is going to come in judgment against the nations of Assyria and Egypt. And it happened. Babylon and Persia triumphed over Assyria. He refers to that judgment as falling upon the *sea*: *"and shall smite the waves in the sea."* Are you beginning to understand what the sea symbolizes? It symbolizes all the Gentile nations, especially those that are around Israel in the eastern Mediterranean area.

Let's look at Ezekiel 26:3, *"Therefore thus saith the Lord God; Behold I am against thee, O Tyrus, and will cause many nations to come up against thee, as the sea causeth his waves to come up."* (Waves here symbolize the individual nations in the sea.)

Tyre was another city/state of its day, formerly Phoenician, now in modern Lebanon. (Tyre and Sidon were the main cities of that old Phoenician Empire.) God says He will cause nations to come against Tyre like the *sea* causes waves.

EZEKIEL 26:4–5

4 And they shall destroy the walls of Tyrus, and break down her towers: I will also scrape her dust from her, and make her like the top of a rock.

5 It shall be a place for the spreading of nets in the midst of the sea: for I have spoken it, saith the Lord God: and it shall become a spoil to the nations.

What God is saying in His Word about Tyre is the same thing he said against Babylon. He will cause other nations to come against the city/state and destroy it. The other nations that came against Tyre are symbolized by the word "sea." (The Phoenicians were overrun by Assyria and finally Greece.)

Daniel's Vision

In Daniel chapter 7, we find Daniel explaining a vision or dream he saw during the first year Belshazzar was king of Babylon. In the morning, he wrote the vision down and told the king about it. Notice that the sea played a prominent role in his vision.

DANIEL 7:2

2 Daniel spake and said, I saw in my vision by night, and, behold, the four winds of the heaven strove [here are the four winds around the earth striving again] upon the great sea.

We know those winds represent things that cause strife on the earth. They strove upon the great sea. Daniel continues his dream.

DANIEL 7:3–7

3 And four great beasts came up from the sea, diverse one from another.

4 The first was like a lion, and had eagle's wings: I beheld till the wings therefore were plucked, and it was lifted up from the earth, and made stand upon the feet as a man, and a man's heart was given to it.

5 And behold another beast, a second, like to a bear, and it raised up itself on one side, and it had three ribs in the mouth of it between the teeth of it: and they said thus unto it, Arise, devour much flesh.

6 After this I beheld, and lo another, like a leopard, which had upon the back of it four wings of a fowl; the beast had also four heads; and dominion was given to it.

7 After this I saw in the night visions, and behold a fourth beast, dreadful and terrible, and strong exceedingly; and it had great iron teeth: it devoured and brake in pieces, and stamped the residue with the feet of it: and it was diverse from all the beasts that were before it; and it had ten horns.

Daniel saw four empires arise. Did they arise out of the ocean? No, every one of them arose from the nations around the Mediterranean Sea.

The first was the Babylonian Empire; the second, the Medo-Persian Empire; the third, the empire of Alexander the Great (the Greek Empire); and the last, the Roman Empire.

Each encompassed its predecessors and became larger than the previous empires, but all arose out of the same part of the world. The sea, then, represents the Gentile nations, particularly around Israel.

I want you to see two more verses in this light. Isaiah 57:20–21 says, *"But the wicked are like the troubled sea, when it cannot rest, whose waters cast up mire and dirt. There is no peace, saith my God, to the wicked."*

Here, God is referring to those who do not know and honor Him. Notice He compares them to *a sea* that's not at rest.

In Isaiah chapter 60, we find a great prophecy concerning what God said He would do for Israel and us today. I know He is going to fulfill this in the day in which we live.

ISAIAH 60:1–5

1 Arise, shine; for thy light is come, and the glory of the Lord is risen upon thee.

2 For, behold, the darkness shall cover the earth, and gross darkness the people [this has already happened]: but the Lord shall arise upon thee, and his glory shall be seen upon thee.

3 And the Gentiles shall come to thy light, and kings to the brightness of thy rising.

4 Lift up thine eyes round about, and see: all they gather themselves together, they come to thee: thy sons shall come from far, and thy daughters shall be nursed at thy side.

5 Then thou shalt see, and flow together, and thine heart shall fear, and be enlarged; because the abundance of the sea shall be converted unto thee, the forces of the Gentiles shall come unto thee.

Notice that *"the abundance of 'the sea' shall be converted."* The Bible is not a book about *fish*. It's a book about *people*. Therefore, when it says, *"the abundance of the sea shall be converted,"* the word "sea" symbolizes in part the people who live in the eastern Mediterranean—the Gentile nations around Israel. The abundance of them shall be converted and believe God. Yes, that hasn't happened yet, but God's Word never fails or returns void.

"The forces of the Gentiles shall come unto thee." We're going to see the fulfillment of that in our day. Do you see what the earth and the sea represent?

What 'Trees' Symbolize

Let's also consider the word "trees." We'll find some answers in the Book of Isaiah.

ISAIAH 61:1, 3

1 The Spirit of the Lord God is upon me; because the Lord hath anointed me to preach good tidings unto the meek; he hath sent me to bind up the brokenhearted, to proclaim liberty to the captives, and the opening of the prison to them that are bound; . . .

3 To appoint unto them that mourn in Zion, to give unto them beauty for ashes, the oil of joy for mourning, the garment of praise for the spirit of heaviness; that they might be called trees of righteousness. . . .

That's what God calls us: *trees of righteousness*. The prophet is talking about people. All trees in scripture do not symbolize believers. However, they do symbolize *men*.

Some trees, such as the oak of Bashan, tall trees, mighty trees, and the cedars of Lebanon, symbolize *leaders*. Jesus is even symbolized as a cedar of Lebanon in several places in the Old Testament, including Ezekiel 17:22–24.

Even regular trees are mentioned in scripture. We are told that all the trees of the field shall clap their hands (Isa. 55:12). Do you expect to see trees clapping their hands? I don't.

If it happens, I'll be the first to admit I was wrong. But what I'm believing for is that all the people who believe God are going to clap their hands. That's what's important to God. They are going to rejoice and see the things of God. That's what He's saying to us.

Scriptural passages referring to trees include Isaiah 10:18–19, 61:3. Ezekiel 20:45–49 refers to the nation of Edom. Trees can also symbolize *believers.*

Description of a King

But now let's look at Ezekiel chapter 31. This is a very interesting passage because it shows that a tree can symbolize different *kinds of men.*

EZEKIEL 31:3–5

3 Behold, the Assyrian was a cedar in Lebanon with fair branches, and with a shadowing shroud, and of an high stature; and his top was among the thick boughs.

4 The waters made him great, the deep set him up on high with her rivers running round about his plants, and sent out her little rivers unto all the trees of the field.

The prophet is talking about a nation, the king of a nation, and the effect he had upon all mankind.

5 Therefore his height was exalted above all the trees of the field [ordinary people], and his boughs were multiplied, and his

branches became long because of the multitude of waters, when he shot forth.

The passage goes on to describe this king. It tells about what made up his kingdom and everything that came under his influence. And it says that judgment will come upon him because he has disobeyed God.

EZEKIEL 31:13–16

13 Upon his ruin shall all the fowls of heaven remain, and all the beasts of the field shall be upon his branches:

14 To the end that none of all the trees by the waters exalt themselves for their height, neither shoot up their top among the thick boughs, neither their trees stand up in their height, all that drink water: for they are all delivered unto death, to the nether parts of the earth, in the midst of the children of men, with them that go down to the pit.

15 Thus saith the Lord God; In the day when he went down to the grave I caused a mourning: I covered the deep for him, and I restrained the floods thereof, and the great waters were stayed: and I caused Lebanon to mourn for him, and all the trees of the field fainted for him.

16 I made the nations to shake at the sound of his fall, when I cast him down to hell with them that descend into the pit: and all the trees of Eden, the choice and best of Lebanon, all that drink water [water symbolizes life], shall be comforted in the nether parts of the earth.

God doesn't send *trees* beneath the earth when their life is over, does He? But that's where people used to go. In the ages before the Resurrection of Jesus Christ, the spirits of righteous and unrighteous people descended into the center of the earth to Sheol, the place of the departed dead.

The righteous were comforted in a place called "Abraham's bosom," and the unrighteous were tormented in a separate place called hell, which was across "a great gulf" from Abraham's bosom.

A description of this is in Luke chapter 16, where Jesus told the story of the righteous beggar and the unrighteous rich man. (See First Peter 3:18–19 and Ephesians 4:8–9.)

Trees symbolize people. The passages we have studied depict trees as different kinds of people.

Symbolic Truth

Always study the context in which you find such passages. If you can see a plain meaning, take it and accept it. Don't argue with it.

But as we look further into the Book of Revelation and see these things being used symbolically, understand that God wants us to know something from these symbols. Believers have the means to understand these things. The Bible contains symbolism that was meant to be understood only by believers. The world does not understand what they mean because the truth is veiled behind this symbolism.

Look for symbolic truths. When you find them, compare them to scripture that uses the same symbolism in its images. Then apply this truth as you read these verses. You will find the use of symbols in God's Word is consistent.

God does not use a symbol in one book to mean one thing and the same symbol in Revelation to mean exactly the opposite. The symbol will mean the same thing in both books—the Bible agrees with itself. God wants us to find the agreement in it and use it. Don't assign symbolic meaning based on whims. That's just the work of the head (1 Cor. 2:13–14), and it doesn't accomplish anything.

Now return to Revelation 7:1 and read the verse with this new understanding. "*And after these things I saw four angels standing on the four comers of the earth, holding the four winds* [or the strife] *of the earth.*"

What they're holding back are the powers, principalities, rulers of darkness in this world, and the spiritual wickedness in high places.

Prayer Power

What do you suppose is causing the angels to do that? As we will see later on, it's the prayers of the saints that cause such things to happen.

God doesn't stand in heaven orchestrating everything that happens on earth all by Himself. He's waiting for people like Daniel, who saw evil conditions in his nation and prayed. God is waiting for us to see what His will is and pray toward it.

Strife is being held back by believers who are praying. God is holding it back in response to their prayers that the winds should not blow, and strife should not envelop Israel, the Gentile nations around Israel, or any of the men in those nations. That's what God said.

REVELATION 7:2–4

2 And I saw another angel ascending from the east, having the seal of the living God: and he cried with a loud voice to the four angels, to whom it was given to hurt the earth [Israel] and the sea [Gentile nations],

3 Saying, Hurt not the earth [Israel], neither the sea [Gentile nations], nor the trees [the leaders or the ordinary men of those nations], till we have sealed the servants of our God in their foreheads.

4 And I heard the number of them which were sealed. . . .

The Jewish Evangelists

From the 12 tribes of Israel, 144,000 will be sealed—12,000 out of each tribe. What are they going to be sealed with? The Holy Spirit. What are they going to do? Preach the Gospel.

Remember the far-reaching effect the Jewish believers of the first century had as soon as they accepted Jesus as Lord? They were mighty preachers of the Gospel, weren't they?

The Bible says that Philip went down to Samaria and preached Christ to the people. They were all amazed, beholding the signs and wonders and receiving the Gospel with great joy (Acts 8).

Then an angel of the Lord spoke to Philip and told him to leave his successful revival and go to the desert. He obeyed and found an Ethiopian reading from the Book of Isaiah as he was riding home from Jerusalem in his chariot. Philip ran up to the chariot at God's direction and asked, "Do you understand what you are reading?" This Ethiopian government official admitted, "No, but who can explain it to me?" Philip replied, "Allow me."

Beginning in Isaiah, Philip preached Christ to the man. Christ can be preached from the knowledge of the Old Testament just as well as from the knowledge of the New Testament. Philip was preaching Christ out of the scriptures of the Old Testament before there was a New Testament.

The People of the Book

Many Jews today, particularly the Orthodox, are experts in the Old Testament. They know it better than you and I could ever think of knowing it. It's head knowledge to them right now. But when a person who loves the Word of God that much gets saved, what becomes of head knowledge? It becomes heart knowledge. And soon, with their enormous zeal for the things of God, a whole group of new believers will spring up.

I believe Orthodox Jews are the most likely to be among the 144,000. However, because they are not the only Jews who know their Bible well, that does not exclude other Jews who will become believers in Jesus Christ as their Messiah.

I've known many Christians who multiplied their effectiveness for God immediately after they were baptized in the Holy Spirit. The same principle will apply to these Jews. When they get hooked up with the Holy Spirit, they will be effective in a hurry.

Many of them, particularly the Orthodox, already know the Old Testament scriptures backwards and forwards, for they have to memorize them from the time they are children and quote them to be received into the community at their Bar Mitzvah when they are 13.

They won't need to be full grown in the knowledge of the New Covenant when they begin to be effective evangelists. They will go right out and start preaching, gaining knowledge as they grow. To me, this is Israel's part in the gleaning of the harvest field. Let's look at that.

Soulwinning Is Harvesting

God always likens people being saved to a harvest. He says we are to pray the Lord of the harvest that He will send forth laborers into His harvest (Matt. 9:38), for the fields are indeed white and ripe unto harvest (John 4:35).

When we look at Leviticus 19:9 and see what God says about the harvest, we can see that He is speaking in types and shadows of what He will do in the future. *"And when ye reap the harvest of your land, thou shall not wholly reap the corners of thy field, neither shalt thou gather the gleanings of thy harvest."*

In other words, you always miss something when you harvest around rocks, trees, and corners, as we discussed before. Gleaners, to this very day, go into the fields after what was left.

When I flew to and from south Florida during years of military service, I saw the tons of tomatoes that were left in the fields after the harvest. You could pick all you wanted. It was the same way when I lived in Maine. After the potato harvest, tons of potatoes were left in the fields. (Modern harvesting machines aren't perfect, and they leave a great deal of good food behind.)

Commandments About Gleaning

In ancient Israel, God commanded that the Jews should not completely reap the corners or gather the gleanings. *"And thou shalt not glean thy vineyard, neither shalt thou gather every grape of thy vineyard; thou shalt leave them for the poor and stranger"* (Lev. 19:10).

We saw the benefits of this policy toward the poor and the stranger in the story of Ruth, the Gentile widow who went to live in Israel with her mother-in-law, Naomi. They were destitute and lived off the gleanings. Boaz, a wealthy kinsman of her late husband, saw Ruth and had compassion on her. He made sure plenty of gleanings were left for her and Naomi to live on. Eventually he married Ruth, and she, a Gentile, became a member of the genealogy of our Lord.

The Promised Harvest

There is much truth we can apply to ourselves and also to Israel from a passage which also speaks of harvest.

HOSEA 6:1–3

1 Come, and let us return unto the Lord: for he hath torn, and he will heal us; he hath smitten, and he will bind us up.
2 After two days will he revive us: in the third day he will raise us up, and we shall live in his sight.
3 Then shall we know, if we follow on to know the Lord: his going forth is prepared as the morning; and he shall come unto us as the rain, as the latter and former rain unto the earth.

Have you ever wondered when you went to bed at night if it would be morning in a few hours? Of course not, because day has followed night every day of your life.

You can know this just as surely. When we follow on to know the Lord, His going forth is prepared as the morning. And He will come unto us as the latter and the former rain unto the earth.

Just as surely as the people of Israel follow on to know Him. Just as surely as Israel enters into the New Covenant and *knows* God, they will take their part in His harvest.

Remember, Joel said he saw a time when the locust, the cankerworm, the caterpillar, and the palmerworm would no longer eat up the harvest. He saw a time when God promised to restore the years those things of evil consumed.

And here's Hosea prophesying about Judah having a harvest in the future. "*Also, O Judah, he hath set an harvest for thee, when I returned the captivity of my people*" (Hos. 6:11).

Now look at Zechariah 8. The prophet is foretelling the future of Israel and Judah, the two kingdoms being brought back together again.

He says in verse 23, "*Thus saith the Lord of hosts; In those days* [the end times] *it shall come to pass, that ten men shall take hold out of all languages of the nations, even shall take hold of the skirt of him that is a Jew, saying, We will go with you: for we have heard that God is with you.*"

The Mosaic Covenant Has Ceased

People haven't done that yet, but Israel hasn't come into the New Covenant yet, either. Some people think God will reinstate the Mosaic Covenant all over again with Israel. He won't. The Jews are still trying to practice it, but the Mosaic Covenant is finished. God will not raise it up again. It's finished because it accomplished its purpose.

Jews who accept Jesus as their Messiah during the Tribulation will enter into the same New Covenant that you and I are already in. We see that in Ezekiel chapter 20. And when they do, they will have a part to play in the end-time harvest, although they will not be the only ones who will do the harvesting.

When they get people saved, those people, in turn, will go and win others. Furthermore, the gleaning work of the Jewish believers will not replace the work the Church did. In fact, it is because the Church *fulfilled* her job on earth, preaching the Gospel to every nation, tribe, tongue, and kindred, that Israel can take her part.

Out of this multitude of new Jewish believers and their converts will come the great multitude that comes out of the Great Tribulation.

The Holy Spirit Will Remain on Earth

This is possible because—even in that time of great judgment, tribulation, and trial—God will still have a testimony in the earth. *The Holy Spirit will still be here.* He will not leave when the Church is caught up. He will still be performing His task on earth of wooing the lost to Christ.

Just think: Will God suddenly turn His back on children who will grow up then just because the Great Tribulation is happening? No, He will not. Psalm 145:9 says, *"His tender mercies are over all His works."* Never will there be a time when that is not true. He will give the people living at the time of the Tribulation the same opportunity to believe that everyone had before the Tribulation and the Rapture.

The vast majority of people who get saved are young people, anyway. Eighty-six percent of all people who get saved are saved before they are 14 years old. The next 10 percent get saved before they are thirty. That means only four percent of the population gets saved after the age of 30.

I was 32 when I got saved. That means I went 96 percent of the way to hell! People's hearts get harder as they grow older, so God deals strongly with the younger generation while they are growing and developing, seeking to win them to Himself.

Patience for the Harvest

God will have a Gospel witness in the earth even in the time of that Great Tribulation, until Jesus returns at the end of the Tribulation with all the saints. These witnesses will be gleaners in His harvest field. He has great patience for the precious fruit of the earth. God will have what He said in His Word.

JAMES 5:7

7 . . . Behold, the husbandman waiteth for the precious fruit of the earth, and hath long patience for it, until he receive the early and latter rain.

Ezekiel 20 covers the same time period that we just read about in Revelation 7.

EZEKIEL 20:33–34

33 As I live, saith the Lord God, surely with a mighty hand, and with a stretched out arm, and with fury poured out, will I rule over you [Israel].

34 And I will bring you out from the people, and will gather you out of the countries wherein ye are scattered, with a mighty hand, and with a stretched out arm, and with fury poured out.

It would seem that the anti-Semitism, the pogroms (massacres), and the Holocaust suffered by the Jews, especially in this century, would fit that description.

A Way of Escape

In 1917, God miraculously opened Palestine, the ancient Jewish homeland, to Jews who wanted to return. The government of Great Britain had a mandate over Palestine. And through the Balfour Declaration, they announced that Jews were welcome to return and live in Palestine if they wished.

Jews who espoused this cause of reclaiming the land were called Zionists. This passionate minority went throughout the world, wherever there were Jewish communities, telling the Jews living there what happened and imploring them to emigrate and reclaim their ancestral homeland. Few caught the vision and returned to the land of their fathers.

Among those who did, however, was the Milwaukee schoolteacher, Golda Meir. She helped pioneer one of the communal settlements, called a kibbutz. Meir later became prime minister of the state of Israel.

Why didn't other Jews leave the countries they were living in and return to Palestine? Shortly after Hitler came to power, the Nazis slammed the door on Jewish emigration, and it became impossible for them to leave Europe. Tragically, after World War II, England changed its policy and denied them entry into Palestine.

After World War II, when people asked the Jews, "Why didn't you leave Europe while you still had the opportunity," they replied, "Well, we had businesses. We had roots. We had families—everything was here."

God had given them a way to escape Hitler's destruction of their people, but most of them didn't take it. God always provides a way of escape. It's not an absolute for all, but if you should ever be faced with some kind of tribulation, there is a way of escape if you will take it.

God's Message to His People

God continued His message to the Jews.

EZEKIEL 20:35–37

35 And I will bring you into the wilderness of the people, and there will I plead with you face to face.

36 Like as I pleaded with your fathers in the wilderness of the land of Egypt, so will I plead with you, saith the Lord God.

37 And I will cause you to pass under the rod, and I will bring you into the bond of the covenant.

"The rod" symbolizes the Word of God. This is why I know this passage applies to the Jewish people today—Israel has never passed under the rod.

David said in Psalm 23:4, *"Thy rod and thy staff they comfort me."* He was talking about God's Word and His Spirit.

When Ezekiel prophesied to the Jews about the covenant in verse 37, they already had a covenant with God. Ezekiel could not have meant the Old Covenant because they were already in it.

The meaning is that God is going to make the Jews submit themselves to His Word, receive Jesus Christ as their Messiah, and bring them into the same New Covenant you and I are in—after He has dealt with them with fury poured out.

God's Fishers and Hunters

In Jeremiah 16:16, God said, "I'm going to send out fishers, and they are going to fish you. Then I'm going to send out hunters, and they are going to hunt you."

A fisherman lures something, doesn't he? God lured the Jews when He reopened their homeland to them in 1917, but they didn't go, so God sent out hunters. Of course, that does not mean God gave Hitler his marching orders, but what happened is what God knew would happen to the Jews. They were driven out of Germany and many other places in Europe where they had lived for hundreds of years.

When the opportunity finally came again to return to Palestine after World War II, tens of thousands took it, entering Palestine illegally if necessary. By then they had little left to keep them in Europe. They were desperate to feel safe in their own country.

The Land of Their Fathers

How many left America at that time? Hardly any. That's the fulfillment of what God was predicting when His prophet said,

EZEKIEL 20:37–44

37 And I will cause you to pass under the rod, and I will bring you into the bond of the covenant:

38 And I will purge out from among you the rebels, and them that transgress against me: I will bring them forth out of the country where they sojourn, and they shall not enter into the land of Israel: and ye shall know that I am the Lord.

39 As for you, O house of Israel, thus saith the Lord God; Go ye, serve ye every one his idols, and hereafter also, if ye will not hearken unto me: but pollute ye my holy name no more with your gifts, and with your idols.

40 For in mine holy mountain [that is, the kingdom of heaven], in the mountain of the height of Israel, saith the Lord God, there shall all the house of Israel, all of them in the land, serve me: [when they come into the New Covenant] there will I accept them, and there will I require your offerings, and the firstfruits of your oblations, with all your holy things.

41 I will accept you with your sweet savour, when I bring you out from the people, and gather you out of the countries wherein ye have been scattered; and I will be sanctified in you before the heathen.

42 And ye shall know that I am the Lord, when I shall bring you into the land of Israel, into the country for the which I lifted up mine hand to give it to your fathers.

43 And there shall ye remember your ways, and all your doings, wherein ye have been defiled; and ye shall lothe yourselves in your own sight for all your evils that ye have committed.

44 And ye shall know that I am the Lord, when I have wrought with you for my name's sake, not according to your wicked ways, nor according to your corrupt doings, O ye house of Israel, saith the Lord God.

God said He is doing this for His Name's sake. He is doing it because He said He would do it. He is doing it to bring His words to pass. This is a new generation. He is dealing with this generation of Jews differently. By His grace, they will come into the New Covenant and become believers in the Messiah. (Ezekiel prophesies further along these lines to the Jewish people in Ezekiel chapters 36 and 37.)

A Worldwide Harvest

In Revelation chapter 7, after we are told about the 144,000 Jews that God is going to take out of the twelve tribes, we are told more about their part in the end-time harvest.

REVELATION 7:9–10, 13–14, 16–17

9 After this I beheld, and, lo, a great multitude, which no man could number, of all nations, and kindreds, and people, and tongues, . .

In other words, the Jewish believers and those they win to the Lord will go out and glean the whole harvest field: not just the nation of Israel—but the entire world.

9 . . . stood before the throne, and before the Lamb, clothed with white robes [that means they are saved], and palms in their hands [that means they are still young in the Lord];

10 And cried with a loud voice, saying, Salvation to our God which sitteth upon the throne, and unto the Lamb. . . .

13 And one of the elders answered, saying unto me, What are these which are arrayed in white robes? and whence came they?

14 And I said unto him, Sir, thou knowest. And he said to me, *These are they which came out of great tribulation, and have washed their robes, and made them white in the blood of the Lamb. . . .*

16 They shall hunger no more, neither thirst any more [they have been through hard times]; neither shall the sun light on them, nor any heat.

17 For the Lamb which is in the midst of the throne shall feed them, and shall lead them unto living fountains of waters: and God shall wipe away all tears from their eyes.

Some people read that and say, "The Church must go through the Great Tribulation." They need to read the rest of the Word and do a little work.

The Church and the Tribulation

The Church is not going through the Great Tribulation. It is not the will of God. If it were, you could endure it, for God would sustain you through it. Instead, it is His will for you and me, the present Gentile Church, to preach the Gospel in all the nations.

After the Church has accomplished this task of harvesting the earth, God will gather her to Himself. Then He will have Israel finish the work of world evangelism, gleaning the harvest fields of the Church. As we have seen, this work is going to be finished by the young Jewish believers and the new converts they win from among the nations.

Palm Branches and Deliverance

We will now turn our attention to Ezekiel chapter 36 and Revelation chapter 7. We have just read about the great multitude that stood before the throne and the Lamb, clothed in white robes (signifying they were saved), holding palm branches in their hands.

An early reference to palm branches is seen in Leviticus chapter 23, when the Feast of Tabernacles was instituted and instructions were given for its celebration.

This weeklong celebration, observed to this day by the worldwide Jewish community, commemorates the deliverance of Israelites out of Egypt. During the week, instead of living in their homes, the people live or at least eat outside in "booths" made with branches. And in these booths, they celebrate deliverance from all kinds of bondage, for Egypt symbolizes the different forms of bondage in the world.

A New Testament reference to palms is seen when Jesus rode into Jerusalem on a colt while the people cheered Him (Matt. 21). They waved palm branches in welcome, believing He was coming as an earthly king to deliver Israel from the bondage of the Roman Empire. (Palm Sunday stems from this event.)

The fact that the new believers are holding palm branches in Revelation 7:9 symbolizes something else. They have been or are anticipating being "delivered" from the world. They are brand new. They are spiritual babies, in a sense. Having just been delivered, they are without a great deal of growth or maturity.

They have been delivered into a time of great tribulation in the earth. That they are clothed in white proves that the work of salvation continues in the earth throughout the Tribulation. We also saw who will be preaching the Gospel and giving the inhabitants of the earth the opportunity to receive the truth.

The "spiritual babies" are the gleanings of the harvest in the field. Revelation 7:9 says they are from "all nations." That indicates they are the fruit of that time period.

Ezekiel's Vision

Now go back to Ezekiel chapter 34 with me. Remember, at the beginning of the seventh chapter of Revelation, we explored what the earth, sea, and trees symbolize. Another good reference about trees is in the following passage that refers to Israel, the Church, and us individually.

EZEKIEL 34:25–28

25 And I will make with them [Israel] a covenant of peace, and will cause the evil beasts to cease out of the land: and they shall dwell safely in the wilderness, and sleep in the woods.

26 And I will make them and the places round about my hill a
blessing; and I will cause the shower to come down in his sea-
son; there shall be showers of blessings.
27 And the tree of the field shall yield her fruit, and the earth shall
yield her increase, and they [the trees of the field and the earth]
shall be safe in their land, and shall know that I am the Lord,
when I have broken the bands of their yoke, and delivered them
out of the hand of those that served themselves of them.
28 And they shall no more be a prey to the heathen, neither shall
the beast of the land devour them; but they shall dwell safely,
and none shall make them afraid.

At the end of this chapter, God calls Israel His "flock," so we know He is talking about men again. Notice that He is especially addressing the nation of Israel here.

We read in Ezekiel 20:33 where God said He would bring His people back into their own land *"with fury poured out,"* and He would do it for His Name's sake (v. 44).

A Prophecy to the Land

In Ezekiel chapter 36, we see these sentiments expressed again and again. Ezekiel begins by delivering a prophecy to the land itself. This is a prophecy spoken to the actual *land* of Israel (known earlier as Palestine).

EZEKIEL 36:1–9

1 Also, thou son of man, prophesy unto the mountains of Israel,
and say, Ye mountains of Israel, hear the word of the Lord:
2 Thus saith the Lord God; Because the enemy hath said against
you, Aha, even the ancient high places are ours in possession:
3 Therefore prophesy and say, Thus saith the Lord God; Because
they have made you desolate, and swallowed you up on every
side, that ye might be a possession unto the residue of the

heathen, and ye are taken up in the lips of talkers, and are an infamy of the people:
4 Therefore ye mountains of Israel, hear the word of the Lord God; Thus saith the Lord God to the mountains, and to the hills, to the rivers, and to the valleys, and to the desolate wastes, and to the cities that are forsaken, which became a prey and derision to the residue of the heathen that are round about;
5 Therefore thus saith the Lord God; Surely in the fire of my jealousy have I spoken against the residue of the heathen, and against all Idumea [Edom] which have appointed my land into their possession with the joy of all their heart, with the despiteful minds, to cast it out for a prey.
6 Prophesy therefore concerning the land of Israel, and say unto the mountains, and to the hills, to the rivers, and to the valleys, Thus saith the Lord God; Behold, I have spoken in my jealousy and in my fury, because ye have borne the shame of the heathen:
7 Therefore thus saith the Lord God; I have lifted up mine hand, Surely the heathen that are about you, they shall bear their shame.
8 But ye, O mountains of Israel, ye shall shoot forth your branches, and yield your fruit to my people of Israel; for they are at hand to come.
9 For, behold, I am for you, and I will tum unto you, and ye shall be tilled and sown.

'Tilled and Sown'

If you looked at Israel before 1948, you know it was a desolate place. Some collective settlements had been started by the Zionists, but for the most part, the land was uninhabited and unproductive.

The first time I saw the modern nation of Israel in the 1950s, it still was that way. The majority of it was a desert, for its once abundant forests had been decimated, particularly under Turkish rule. Malaria-ridden swamps encircled the Sea of Galilee.

But look at it today. The desert has blossomed. What God said has already come to pass in that respect. The Jews have made a fertile land out of Israel. Seemingly, the land responded only to their touch.

The Jews became experts at irrigating and fertilizing their land, particularly the desert, and it is yielding tremendous crops. God has already tilled and sown Israel.

In fact, the Israelis grow more fruit and vegetables than they can consume. They are one of the few nations on earth that can export their excess to the markets of the world. Fresh produce and flowers from Israel are sold daily in the marketplaces of Europe—produce that originated in a former desert.

The People Return

Ezekiel 36:10 begins, *"And I will multiply men upon you."* Before World War II, few Jews remained in Israel. God had promised He would multiply men upon that land, and He's doing it. After World War II, a tremendous exodus of Jews came from Europe and Asia. Since then, there has been a steady stream of immigrants. At the time of this writing, Russian Jews, long limited from emigrating, are now flooding into their ancient homeland, prompting worries about housing and unemployment among the Jews already in Israel.

Verse 10 continues, *"all the house of Israel, even all of it: and the cities shall be inhabited, and the wastes shall be builded."*

Some people who teach about end times say the only tribe God is dealing with anymore is Judah, for He has forsaken the rest of the tribes of Israel. That's not what He says here. He says *all* of Israel. All of them. The whole nation.

Verse 11, *"And I will multiply upon you man and beast; and they shall increase and bring fruit: and I will settle you after your old estates, and will do better unto you than at your beginnings: and ye shall know that I am the Lord."*

When this happens, the Jews will know God the way we know Him under the New Covenant. This hasn't happened yet. As we read this prophecy to the land of Israel further, we will see what has happened and what is about to happen in Israel.

EZEKIEL 36:13–20

13 Thus saith the Lord God; Because they say unto you, Thou land devourest up men, and hast bereaved thy nations;
14 Therefore thou shalt devour men no more, neither bereave thy nations any more, saith the Lord God.
15 Neither will I cause men to hear in thee the shame of the heathen any more, neither shalt thou bear the reproach of the people any more, neither shalt thou cause thy nations to fall any more, saith the Lord God.
16 Moreover the word of the Lord came unto me, saying,
17 Son of man, when the house of Israel dwelt in their own land, they defiled it by their own way and by their doings: their way was before me as the uncleanness of a removed woman.
18 Wherefore I poured my fury upon them for the blood that they had shed upon the land, and for their idols wherewith they had polluted it:
19 And I scattered them among the heathen, and they were dispersed through the countries: according to their way and according to their doings I judged them.
20 And when they entered unto the heathen, whither they went, they profaned my holy name, when they said to them, These are the people of the Lord, and are gone forth out of his land.

Natural Seed and Spiritual Seed

You see, there are two types of Jews. Those who come naturally from the line of Abraham, Isaac, and Jacob. (Other natural descendants of Abraham are the Arabs, but we're studying about Israel here.)

Then there are those who are the spiritual "seed" the New Testament mentions. Galatians 3:29 says, *"And if ye be Christ's, then are ye Abraham's seed, and heirs according to the promise."*

God, speaking to Abraham, said in Genesis 22:17, *"That in blessing I will bless thee, and in multiplying I will multiply thy seed as the stars of the heaven, and as the sand which is upon the sea shore; and thy seed shall possess the gate of his enemies."* The "sand of the sea" symbolizes the *natural seed* of Abraham, but the "stars of the heaven" symbolize his *spiritual seed* (those who believe in Jesus).

The Apostle Paul said he was from both lines: born a Jew from the natural seed and born again as a believer in the Messiah, becoming spiritual seed. There are those today, like Paul, who are both. Any Jew who desires to be from both lines can be.

In Ezekiel 36:19, the prophet talks about the natural seed having their natural way—their religion, if you will. God said they defiled the land and polluted it with their idols (v. 18).

This sounds like some of the pointed things Jesus said to the Pharisees in His day. He told them, "You say Abraham is your father, but if he was, you would believe Me. But you don't believe Me. You are of your father—the devil." (See John 8:39–44.)

There are two types of people God is addressing over and over again in scripture—the natural seed and the spiritual seed of Abraham.

When you see the word "Israel," you must always look at it in context to determine which group God is referring to.

The prophet Ezekiel said the natural seed went out into all the nations and misrepresented Him.

EZEKIEL 36:22–23

22 Therefore say unto the house of Israel, Thus saith the Lord God; I do not this for your sakes, O house of Israel, but for mine holy name's sake, which ye have profaned among the heathen, whither ye went.

23 And I will sanctify my great name, which was profaned among the heathen, which ye have profaned in the midst of them; and the heathen shall know that I am the Lord, saith the Lord God, when I shall be sanctified in you before their eyes.

God said He had pity on the natural seed for the sake of His holy Name. They thought, "We are the people of God." God has no natural people in a sense that He's more concerned about them than He is about someone else. What He said in this passage is that people's *carnal* doings are an abomination to Him.

Does God Have Favorites?

God favors some people all right, but whom does He favor? Believers. People who believe. He can favor people who believe—He does and He should. This He said He would do, but He doesn't favor one natural group over any other natural group.

During the Great Tribulation when God brings the natural Jews into the New Covenant we're living in—as we saw in Ezekiel 20:37, and they pass under the rod and submit themselves to the Word of God—they will be sanctified before the eyes of the heathen.

They are going to believe and trust in Jesus. They are going to realize Jesus Christ was their Messiah. And are they ever going to make up for lost time.

EZEKIEL 36:24

24 For I will take you from among the heathen, and gather you out of all countries, and will bring you into your own land.

Someone may ask, "Do you believe that verse has to do with believers?" Certainly it does. You can apply it to yourself as an individual, or you can apply it to the Church as a body. And you can apply it to the ones it was addressed to: Israel. That's who God is talking to.

We quote the next few verses about ourselves all the time, and that's all right, because they do apply to us. But don't fail to see how they applied to the people God originally addressed them to.

EZEKIEL 36:25

25 Then will I sprinkle clean water upon you, and ye shall be clean: from all your filthiness, and from all your idols, will I cleanse you.

Religion is nothing but idolatry. It doesn't make any difference what name is on it. God has no favorite religion. Everything done in the name of their religion, Judaism, is past.

The Jews are trying to keep a covenant that was finished almost two thousand years ago. God said it was finished, but the Jews are still trying to live by it, and their efforts are their own works. God is not stirring them to keep the Old Covenant. That's their own doing. He wants to teach them a better way. But He has said things concerning the nation of Israel that will come to pass.

No matter what the Jewish people have done, these things will come to pass.

A New Heart, A New Spirit

EZEKIEL 36:26–31

26 A new heart also will I give you, and a new spirit will I put within you: and I will take away the stony heart out of your flesh, and I will give you an heart of flesh.
27 And I will put my spirit within you, and cause you to walk in my statutes, and ye shall keep my judgments, and do them.
28 And ye shall dwell in the land that I gave to your fathers; and ye shall be my people, and I will be your God.
29 I will also save you from all your uncleannesses: and I will call for the corn, and will increase it, and lay no famine upon you.
30 And I will multiply the fruit of the tree, and the increase of the field, that ye shall receive no more reproach of famine among the heathen.
31 Then shall ye remember your own evil ways, and your doings that were not good, and shall lothe yourselves in your own sight for your iniquities and for your abominations.

That's true repentance, isn't it? God says they will be repentant about the religion they have been practicing.

EZEKIEL 36:32

32 Not for your sakes do I this, saith the Lord God, be it known unto you: be ashamed and confounded for your own ways, O house of Israel.

God says, "It's not because you're a favored nation or because you have pleased Me somehow. No, not for your sakes do I do these things."

The Second Regathering

EZEKIEL 36:33–38

33 Thus saith the Lord God; In the day that I shall have cleansed you from all your iniquities I will also cause you to dwell in the cities, and the wastes shall be builded.

34 And the desolate land shall be tilled, whereas it lay desolate in the sight of all that passed by.

35 And they shall say, This land that was desolate is become like the garden of Eden; and the waste and desolate and ruined cities are become fenced, and are inhabited.

36 Then the heathen that are left round about you shall know that I the Lord build the ruined places, and plant that that was desolate: I the Lord have spoken it, and I will do it.

37 Thus saith the Lord God; I will yet for this be enquired of by the house of Israel, to do it for them; I will increase them with men like a flock.

38 As the holy flock, as the flock of Jerusalem in her solemn feasts; so shall the waste cities be filled with flocks of men: and they shall know that I am the Lord.

Some people will contend, "God already did that when He regathered the Jews out of their Babylonian captivity."

No, this passage is not talking about the Babylonian regathering. You see in Isaiah 11:11 where God said He would put forth His hand and gather the children of Israel again the second time. This passage is describing that second regathering.

Many Jews never returned to Israel from their Babylonian captivity. They remained (and remain) scattered throughout the world. Others returned and are still returning, as we have seen, in this century.

But God said He is going to bring them all back to their homeland, and He is going to do it. It will come to pass. I am emphasizing this because some people who teach about the end times say this prophecy has no application whatsoever to the nation of Israel. Such people would have to have a very low regard for the Word of God to say or believe that.

What God says plainly, you must understand plainly. If God says such-and-such means a certain thing, who are we to say it doesn't? It must mean what it says. God cannot lie and does not tell lie to illustrate spiritual truths.

This passage illustrates a spiritual truth to us. We know we have a new heart. We know we have been recipients of the Holy Spirit. We know Ezekiel was prophesying to us as well. We know that. What we need to be schooled in is the fact that God means exactly what He says, and He will do what He says He will do.

Ezekiel's Allegory

Ezekiel chapter 37 is an allegory about Israel coming together again. Ezekiel just goes back and states it a different way, using the vivid example of a valley of dry bones.

God tells him, "Watch and prophesy to them and see what happens." So Ezekiel prophesies over the bones, and all of a sudden, the bones start coming together. First the bones, then the flesh appeared. They were joined together like men.

The point is, *natural* prosperity comes before *spiritual* prosperity. We can see an example of this in the Kingdom of Esau. It was firmly established and flourishing before the Kingdom of Jacob ever took hold. Esau had a mighty kingdom before Israel was a nation, but where is Esau's kingdom today? It's scattered—eaten up by the nations around it.

And where is Israel? It's still there. The Jews are the only people I know of who have returned to their homeland after having been scattered throughout the whole world for nearly 2,000 years. God said the Jews would return to Israel, and they are returning. He is going to fulfill all the promises He made to Israel.

Dry Bones Live Again

In chapter 37 the bones came together, flesh appeared, and then sinew. In other words, the natural man was recreated. After this happened, what did God do? He breathed life into the body, and it stood and walked again.

You can see the bones of Israel have come together again. You can see the flesh has appeared on the bones, and the body has been recreated, so to speak. In the natural, they are in their land again. But the life that God said He would breathe into them hasn't come yet. It's coming, but they haven't received it yet. It's even there in their midst.

Did you know there are Christians who live in Israel just to pray for the Jews and be a witness to them? They must depend on the Holy Spirit when sharing the Good News, especially in Israel. Jewish people have to see something they want. Something must happen to turn their attitude from the way it has been toward Christians.

I can't blame them for not trusting us after all the persecution they have suffered at the hands of so-called Christians throughout the centuries. They've been blamed for everything from the crucifixion of Jesus to financial problems on the stock exchange.

Today, the Christian Embassy in Jerusalem and other Christian ministries located in Israel are praying for that nation and showing the Jewish people the love of God, and they are beginning to respond.

Before the Church finishes its time on the earth, the Jews are going to see things that will make them jealous of what we have. They are going to know that we have a relationship with their God and not just a relationship but fellowship as well.

From that realization of what they are missing, they will repent and see where they've missed it. There will be one last great testimony on the earth. To me that will be the catching away of the Church. When the Jews see us go to be with their God, they are going to be jealous.

Ezekiel chapter 37 depicts this future turning to God plainly, although you can see how it could apply to the Church as well.

EZEKIEL 37:21–22

21 . . . Behold, I will take the children of Israel from among the heathen, whither they be gone, and will gather them on every side, and bring them into their own land:

22 And I will make them one nation in the land upon the mountains of Israel; and one king shall be king to them all: and they shall be no more two nations, neither shall they be divided into two kingdoms any more at all.

The king who will rule over them is Jesus!

Chapter 4

The Trumpets Sound

Now let's examine the eighth chapter of Revelation. Chronology is not all-important to us here because John keeps referring to the same things over and over again. Whatever is discussed in chapter 6 doesn't necessarily follow what is in chapter 5, and the events in chapter 8 don't necessarily follow chapter 7.

Even though chronology isn't too important, people often get "hung up" on it. They want to predict exactly what is going to happen next. This is a trap you can fall into quite easily. I've fallen into it myself.

You don't need to predict what happens next. And when you try to place dates on all the events you're discussing, you're really sticking your neck out a long way. Good luck to you if you set dates. I hope you have better luck than all the others who have done it. Almost everyone who has ever tried to place dates on these events in Revelation has failed, so why would you want to join that crowd?

The Seventh Seal

In Revelation 8:1, we read: *"And when he had opened the seventh seal, . . ."* He who opens the seventh seal is Jesus, the Lamb of God, who also opened the first six. The seven trumpets begin to sound as this seventh seal is opened, and they sound in order. After the seventh trumpet, we will see the seven vials of wrath poured out, or opened.

REVELATION 8:1

1 And when he had opened the seventh seal, there was silence in heaven about the space of half an hour.

You might say we're getting a broader look in chapter 8 at what happens before and during the time Jesus referred to as the Great Tribulation.

All the created beings in heaven are in awe. We've come to the end of this age. We've come to the point in time when Jesus Christ will return to reign on earth.

Everything that happened since the time of Adam has pointed toward this time. God is fulfilling and completing everything He said He would. It's all coming to a point or climax ahead.

God's Symphony

The Father is not in a hurry, however, because He is never in a hurry. He won't be in a hurry the day before Jesus comes for the Church, either. That's because all this is already orchestrated in heaven.

The Father is the Conductor who prepared the score. We are the musicians He will lead in the great performance of it. As we have seen, Israel will join in for the final movement of that symphony.

REVELATION 8:2–3

2 And I saw the seven angels which stood before God; and to them were given seven trumpets.

3 And another angel came and stood at the altar, having a golden censer; and there was given unto him much incense, that he should offer it with the prayers of all saints upon the golden altar which was before the throne.

As you can see, the saints' prayers are still having an effect. The prayers you prayed here on the earth are still having an effect on that day. The prayers that are prayed in that day will also have an effect.

REVELATION 8:4–5

4 And the smoke of the incense, which came with the prayers of the saints, ascended up before God out of the angels' hand.
5 And the angel took the censer, and filled it with fire of the altar, and cast it into the earth: and there were voices, and thunderings, and lightnings, and an earthquake.

The actions of this angel show that earthshaking spiritual things are still happening on the planet Earth.

The 144,000 Jewish believers are doing the work God has sealed them to do. Holy Spirit fire of salvation, healing, and deliverance has been cast onto the earth. The word "earth" as used here is first a reference to Israel because, as we saw in Revelation chapter 7, the focus of faith in the world is now on that nation above all other nations.

Mercy and Judgment

The opening of the seventh seal by the Lamb of God initially shows that mercy and grace can still be received by all who will receive it.

The works of God related in Revelation chapter 7 are shown to be tied from the sixth to the seventh seal. However, it will also be seen that judgment in increasing measure and severity begins to occur upon the world system and the works of the flesh. The next verses relate the details of that judgment.

REVELATION 8:6–7

6 And the seven angels which had the seven trumpets prepared themselves to sound.

7 The first angel sounded, and there followed hail and fire mingled with blood, and they were cast upon the earth: and the third part of trees was burnt up, and all green grass was burnt up.

This is signifying a war that will greatly affect Israel. It is probably a war with her immediate neighbors, and it will have a catastrophic effect upon the nation. The Israelis have been trusting in natural means and their own wisdom and strength to a large degree until this time. These natural defenses are going to be greatly afflicted and affected when this first trumpet sounds.

The Judgment of Hailstones

Hail has often been seen in scripture to be a judgment from God. For example, Joshua was leading the armies of Israel, chasing the five Amorite kings and their armies. Toward the end of that battle, great hailstones fell on the Amorites, and they lost (Joshua 10:8–11). That was recognized as a judgment from God.

In Revelation 16:21, we find a point where, in the coming wrath of God, great hailstones from heaven will fall upon those who are blaspheming God. It is said that these hailstones will weigh as much as 126 pounds, which is the equivalent of a biblical "talent." Imagine a hailstone like that. It represents God's judgment.

One judgment that came upon Egypt prior to the Exodus was hailstones (Exod. 9:22–24).

To summarize: This is a war that suddenly envelops the earth. The use of the word "earth" here is symbolic. It does not refer to the whole earth, just Israel. Some men of that nation (trees) are destroyed. With great bloodshed, the green grass—the youth or militia of that nation—is lost. These resources make up the natural strength the nation has been trusting in. The arm of flesh fails Israel.

Gog and Magog

REVELATION 8:8

8 And the second angel sounded, and as it were a great mountain burning with fire was cast into the sea: and the third part of the sea became blood.

Mountains symbolize nations, coalitions of nations, or great nations. In Ezekiel chapters 38 and 39, God foretells a time when a great coalition of nations led by Gog and Magog (Russia) will invade the Middle East.

Two other nations that are still in existence today, Libya and Ethiopia, will join them. Togarmah is probably Turkey and the surrounding regions. Persia is modern Iran. And Gomer is probably some of the European nations (Ezek. 38:5–6).

There are many reasons these nations would want to invade the Middle East. First is a military reason. The Middle East is a critical location. Every man who has ever tried to conquer the world has recognized the strategic importance of that region and has known he had to control it to achieve world conquest.

Also, oil is in the Middle East. Other parts of the world are running short of oil all the time. For example, Russia is presently running short on its oil supply, so it is becoming more dependent on Middle Eastern oil.

Another reason Israel is such a prize is that it has become a "breadbasket" to the world. It's one of the few nations on earth that produces so much food it can export the excess.

Russia has had a sorry history of crop failures for decades. All her five-year plans have failed. She cannot produce enough food to feed her people. Russia has been dependent on other nations for food for years and doesn't like it. And she has already made plans to invade the Middle East.

In 1982, Israel went into Lebanon, capturing Tyre and Sidon, those ancient Phoenician cities that are now a part of modern Lebanon. The Israelis discovered vast supplies of Russian weapons and ammunition that had been stockpiled by Russia and her allies (most likely the PLO) toward the day when they would invade the Middle East.

The ever practical Israelis called for every available truck in Israel. They trucked back all the supplies they could and destroyed the rest.

The Russian plan went awry, but from it, you can see her intent. Russia intends to invade the Middle East. And Russians don't readily change their minds. I've seen what they do to people who are in league with them. They don't keep their word. You might as well make a deal with the devil! If you expect him to keep his word, you could expect them to keep theirs.

A Kingdom Burns

Something dramatic is going to happen on the world scene. It is an invasion of the Middle East, and it is foretold in Revelation 8:8, *"A great mountain burning with fire was cast into the sea."*

What meaning did we establish for the symbolic word "sea"? That region of the world—the Gentile nations that are around Israel.

If you are going to invade Israel, you must go through these nations. No nation on earth is capable of invading another entirely by air. They begin or launch attacks by air, but much of their men and material must come over land and/or sea.

That mountain burning with fire is a kingdom. Ezekiel chapters 38 and 39 (especially chapter 38) clearly tell us where that kingdom comes from. It is Russia and the nations aligned with her.

A picture of that coming invasion is found in Ezekiel 39. It tells of a great coalition (mountain) led by Gog and Magog, which is Russia. Meshech and Tubal, mentioned in Ezekiel 38:2, are tribes that descended from Noah and moved North. There is still a city in Russia called Tobolsk. Meshech is really Moscow.

Let's insert a note of caution here. Because we know from scripture what will happen to these nations in the future, does that mean God has written off these nations. For example, is He through with Iran? No, He's not. Is He through with Russia? No, He's not. Is He through with Libya? No, He's not.

It would be wrong for us to think that because we know what's going to happen in the future, we should write those places off and not consider them fields for evangelization. We would certainly miss the will of God if we did. One reason is that God is moving mightily in Russia and other nations today. He isn't done with any nation because He said He would have a people out of every nation (Rev. 5:9).

Russia's Mistake: Opposing God

The point in time when God has finished the work of harvesting Russia and her allies, that nation is going to make a big mistake. She is going to come down and attack what God is doing. And anytime you oppose what God is doing, you find yourself in the path of divine judgment.

Most of the first trumpets are things people have brought on themselves simply by not doing what God is doing and by putting themselves in opposition to a mighty work of the Holy Spirit.

King Sennacherib of Assyria found out what it means to be opposed to a mighty work of the Holy Spirit. The angel of the Lord slew 185,000 in the camp of the Assyrian army in one night (2 Kings 19:32–37.)

Beware! No man can stand in flesh contrary to the mighty manifestation of the Holy Spirit unless he wants to exit this world early.

The fact that men put themselves in opposition to what God was doing and what He said He would do is why the great judgments come.

Here, the armies come—that great mountain burning with fire—marching right through the Middle East, and it is cast into the sea! *"And the third part of the sea became blood"* (Rev. 8:8). A great war breaks out.

REVELATION 8:9

9 And the third part of the creatures which were in the sea, and had life, died; and the third part of the ships were destroyed.

A third of mankind in the Middle Eastern Gentile nations die.

I don't know what ships symbolize, other than sources of life. We sing about "the old Gospel ship." Where would we be without that ship? We symbolize ourselves as believers that way. This warfare may have an impact on believers in that part of the world who were saved by the work of the 144,000.

A close look at Ezekiel 38:18–39:10 will show that the arm of the flesh failed Israel. God will now rescue the nation supernaturally from the great invasion led by Gog and Magog. His rescue comes when Israel is utterly helpless to do anything to save themselves.

We—who can see into these future events by the Spirit of God—have a responsibility to pray them into existence while we are here.

Pharisees at Work

As the next two trumpets are sounding, we are going to see the work of religious people who are trying to stop what God is doing through the 144,000.

When the devil sees anything going on that God is doing, he always comes against it and uses whatever means he has. If he can stir up a war, he'll stir up a war. If he can't succeed with that, he'll stir up the religious people, the modern-day Pharisees.

We are going to see something that will happen during the time when there will still be a Gospel witness on the earth. The Jewish believers who have been sealed are going forth and preaching. The enemy has begun his opposition by raising up what he can to stop the work of the Lord, if possible, through wars and invasions.

REVELATION 8:10–11

10 And the third angel sounded, and there fell a great star from heaven, burning as it were a lamp, and it fell upon the third part of the rivers, and upon the fountains of water;

11 And the name of the star is called Wormwood: and the third part of the waters became wormwood; and many men died of the waters, because they were made bitter.

A Falling Star

A star is falling from heaven, but it is not a literal star that is going to destroy the world upon impact. It is a symbolic star. What do stars symbolize? Angels.

Throughout the Word of God, stars symbolize either godly angels or fallen angels. In this case, I believe it's a fallen angel, and it's not from God's heaven, but from the heavenlies around the earth.

Think about what happened when Jesus preached the Gospel in His day. Who started reacting to Him and His message? It was the Pharisees, wasn't it? These religious people not only rejected the Gospel, they also began to strive and plot against it.

In the natural sense, they were fairly successful. They prevented many in Israel from receiving the truth. Paul said only a remnant was saved in his day. Tradition can have a strong effect against the preaching of the Gospel.

The name of this star, this angelic being, is Wormwood because it is poisonous and dangerous. It is something that will bring death instead of life. This great star falling from the heavenlies is burning *"as it were a lamp,"* but it's not a lamp. It's just claiming to be a lamp, claiming to be enlightening.

Interestingly, Paul warns believers against this very thing at the beginning of the Church Age. In Colossians chapter 2, he points out that religious men motivated by evil spirits oppose and fight the preaching of the Gospel. And they still do today.

Here in Revelation chapter 8, we see a deception that is being formed against the revival that God has brought forth in Israel. A religious movement will try to stop what God is doing in Israel, much like the Pharisees did to stop Jesus.

The False Prophet

This movement will be headed by the man we call "the False Prophet." This is the first place you meet him. You'll see him again in chapter 13. He's going to be a man who holds both civil and religious authority in the nation of Israel.

He will mislead and misguide the Jews by putting them in an alliance with the Antichrist. This is what will happen in the natural realm: The nation will be misguided by this man.

Paul warns believers of this very thing. What did he tell these believers?

COLOSSIANS 2:4–6

4 And this I say, lest any man should beguile you with enticing words.
5 For though I be absent in the flesh, yet am I with you in the spirit, joying and beholding your order, and the stedfastness of your faith in Christ.
6 As ye have therefore received Christ Jesus the Lord, so walk ye in him.

Paul is saying, "You received Jesus by grace through faith so walk that same way."

COLOSSIANS 2:7–10

7 Rooted and built up in him, and stablished in the faith, as ye have been taught, abounding therein with thanksgiving.
8 Beware lest any man spoil you through philosophy and vain deceit, after the tradition of men, after the rudiments of the world, and not after Christ.
9 For in him dwelleth all the fulness of the Godhead bodily.
10 And ye are complete in him, which is the head of all principality and power.

Paul continues his warning.

COLOSSIANS 2:16

16 Let no man therefore judge you in meat, or in drink, or in respect of an holyday, or of the new moon, or of the sabbath days.

You can see how the Jewish influence was strong in Colossae. Judaizers came into their midst and tried to persuade those believers to go back into a system of works under Jewish law again.

These men attempting to proselyte didn't really understand the Old Covenant themselves. They didn't keep their covenant by faith. They thought they were keeping it by doing works. Jesus had some sharp words for them, especially in John chapter 8, as He dealt with this error of the Pharisees.

Deceived

The same thing that happened in Colossae is happening in Israel during the end times. The devil is trying to stop what God began.

Men are being negatively affected by false doctrine. Someone with a powerful influence is causing men who have heard the Word to fall away from the truth. They are being deceived.

They are symbolized in Revelation 8:10 by *what they could have been.* They once were rivers and fountains of water. But now they are poisoned rivers and poisoned fountains of water. As we look in the Book of John, we see what Jesus promised to those who heard and applied the Word of God.

JOHN 4:14

14 But whosoever drinketh of the water that I shall give him shall never thirst; but the water that I shall give him shall be in him a well of water springing up unto everlasting life.

JOHN 7:38
38 He that believeth on me, as the scripture hath said, out of his belly shall flow rivers of living water.

"A well of water springing up unto everlasting life" and *"rivers of living water"* are what these people would have been if they had not been deceived.

A fallen angel from the heavenlies, part of the spiritual wickedness in high places, is the being who is causing their waters to be poisoned.

A man, the False Prophet, is being used to lead the movement and other men who are following him, much like the Pharisees did in Jesus' day.

"Wormwood" is the name given to that spirit being—and to the effects of what he is doing:

REVELATION 8:11
11 And the name of the star is called Wormwood: and the third part of the waters became wormwood; and many men died of the waters, because they were made bitter.

"Wormwood" in Hebrew is *la'anah*, which means "to curse; poisonous." The word suggests calamity, disaster, and sorrow and is used several times that way in the Old Testament.

The Greek word for "wormwood" is *apsinthion*, which means "bitter, deleterious, or destructive."

Men will be negatively affected by false doctrine. They will be turned away from the truth, and they won't do what God had called them to do. You might say they become neutralized by false doctrine.

Do you see anything like that happening in the Church today? Since it is, you know it can happen in the future too. What's the cure for it? The followers of men's traditions must forsake their deception and accept the Word of God.

How the Work of God Will Be Corrupted

The movement that surfaces in Revelation will be a quick work involving heavy persecution against believers because of the situation they are living in. Latter-day Judaizers will corrupt what God is doing in Israel to a degree.

The Word of God tells us what that degree is—a third of the rivers and waters will be neutralized or fall away.

Remember the star that fell was burning like a torch. Wormwood claims to be enlightening, but he isn't. He actually brings spiritual darkness and bondage with him.

The False Prophet will preach a humanistic peace and will ally Israel with her enemies and the Antichrist. He will denounce the Messianic Jews, saying they are in error when they actually have the truth.

REVELATION 8:12
12 And the fourth angel sounded, and the third part of the sun was smitten, and the third part of the moon, and the third part of the stars; so as the third part of them was darkened, and the day shone not for a third part of it, and the night likewise.

That could be seen as a natural occurrence, but it's really showing the effects of the persecution against believers. *A third of those who could have been involved in the work of God will not be.* The light that would have come from them is darkened. The Gospel light is going to be diminished at that time by what Wormwood and the False Prophet are doing.

Chapter 5

Divine Judgment Increases

John warns his readers of judgment coming in even greater measure.

REVELATION 8:13–9:1

13 And I beheld, and heard an angel flying through the midst of heaven, saying with a loud voice, Woe, woe, woe, to the inhabiters of the earth by reason of the other voices of the trumpet of the three angels, which are yet to sound!

1 And the fifth angel sounded, and I saw a star fall from heaven unto the earth. . . .

Again, this is not a literal star falling from the heavens above us. It is an angel.

The Bottomless Pit

REVELATION 9:1

1 . . . and to him was given the key of the bottomless pit.

Control of the bottomless pit is in the hands of Jesus! He said of Himself:

REVELATION 1:18

18 . . . I am alive for evermore, Amen; and have the keys of hell and of death.

In His resurrection, triumphing over principalities and powers, Jesus got control over this place. The bottomless pit is part of Hades, part of the underworld. In it are imprisoned most evil angels, or fallen spirit beings.

REVELATION 9:2–3

2 And he opened the bottomless pit; and there arose a smoke out of the pit, as the smoke of a great furnace; and the sun and the air were darkened by reason of the smoke of the pit.

3 And there came out of the smoke locusts upon the earth: and unto them was given power, as the scorpions of the earth have power.

Again, this is an allegory, or symbolic statement. The bottomless pit is not a hole in the earth. I've heard all kinds of suppositions about where this bottomless pit is. Some think it's under the Great Pyramid in Egypt. Others think it's in the middle of some exotic land like Iran. Everyone seems to have an opinion about its location.

It's under the earth—that's where it is. It's probably in the middle of the earth if it's bottomless. And it's where fallen angels are imprisoned.

It doesn't make any difference if a hole is in the center of the earth.

Strange Creatures from Inner Space?

Some people have speculated about what kind of beings are released from the pit, based on the description John gave of them. That's not a safe way to interpret the Bible.

What you *think* John saw is not going to interpret the Bible safely or correctly. Instead, you must find something in the Word that agrees with what is happening in these verses.

What would be in the bottomless pit? What's imprisoned in Hades? The spirits of unjust beings, or fallen angels. There are no spirits of *human beings* in the bottomless pit. It contains the spirits of *fallen angels*—angels that have been separated from God for ages and ages.

We can read more about them in First Peter chapter 2 and Jude. Spirits that didn't keep their first estate are imprisoned here under chains of darkness. Some are loosed at different times in scripture, but the entire population of the pit is going to be loosed upon the earth at this point in Revelation 9. Why?

The Judgment of Blasphemers

The ninth chapter of Revelation is the best example I can think of in scripture to prove that men can have what they say—negatively.

During this time, the Gospel will go forth through the 144,000 Jewish believers, but there will be many who will reject it and continually blaspheme God. We see this in the following verses.

REVELATION 9:20–21

20 And the rest of the men which were not killed by these plagues yet repented not of the works of their hands, that they should not worship devils, and idols of gold, and silver, and brass, and stone, and of wood: which neither can see, nor hear, nor walk:

21 Neither repented they of their murders, nor of their sorceries, nor of their fornication, nor of their thefts.

These men are going to bring more and more judgment upon themselves. When we look at this in detail, we will find that the judgment is coming upon those who don't repent. It's coming upon those who blaspheme God. And it's coming in greater measure than it has ever come before in the history of the world. Men *will* have what they say, whether it's good or bad.

Supernatural Wickedness

Why is it that this pit, which has never been opened, is going to be opened at this time? Because men are going to be worse, more evil, and more wicked than they've ever been before. This may be difficult for you to imagine because of the things you may have seen or experienced in the present time, but it *is* going to get worse.

That's one of the signs we're living in the end of the age. The evil are going to get worse and worse, and the godly are going to become better and better. And the distinction between them is becoming clearer all the time.

You can't walk with one foot in both camps any longer. It's plain to see which camp is which. And it's getting easier all the time to differentiate between the Church and the world. That separation is going to continue.

I like what Lester Sumrall said about it. "The Bible predicts that the Church is going to become more and more glorious, but it also predicts that the evil are going to become more and more wicked" (2 Tim. 3:1–5, 13). And that is beginning to be seen.

There will even be a great supernatural manifestation of wickedness because of the evil deeds of men. This release of fallen angels from the pit is part of it.

We read in Revelation 9:3 that *"there came out of the smoke locusts upon the earth."* In other words, there will be so many evil spirits coming out of the pit, they will resemble a great cloud.

What do locusts do? In the natural they destroy harvests, don't they? The enemy is going to try to stop what God is doing, even at the gleaning stage of that harvest.

Power To Torment

REVELATION 9:3

3 . . . and unto them was given power, as the scorpions of the earth have power.

A scorpion has the power to sting with nerve poison. In some cases, people may die from its bite, depending on what kind of scorpion it is. A scorpion bite affects your nervous system. You hurt all over, not just where it bit you. You are in great pain and suffering. And that's what these evil spirits have the power to do—to cause great pain and suffering to humanity.

REVELATION 9:4

4 And it was commanded them that they should not hurt the grass of the earth, neither any green thing, neither any tree; but only those men which have not the seal of God in their foreheads.

"The grass of the earth" and "any green thing" represent young people, or children who have not yet reached the age of accountability. "Any tree" symbolizes the righteous or the upright.

Notice who is going to be bothered or tormented: *"only those men which have not the seal of God in their foreheads."* That's who is going to be affected—those who are blaspheming. Those who are rejecting God.

The fallen angels are going to come out of the pit and torment them. That's why I stated you can have what you say. One way or the other, you can have what you say.

Creatures From the Pit

The fallen angels come up out of the bottomless pit and are restricted by one limitation. As we read on, remember this. These are *spirit beings* who are coming out of the bottomless pit. That's the only kind of creature that is in the bottomless pit.

REVELATION 9:5–6

5 And to them it was given that they should not kill them, but that they should be tormented five months: and their torment was as the torment of a scorpion, when he striketh a man.

6 And in those days shall men seek death, and shall not find it; and shall desire to die, and death shall flee from them.

The same evil spirit that will afflict a man can make him a coward. He would like to kill himself, but he can't find enough courage to do it. From this, we see the enemy manipulate thoughts and acts in the lives of nonbelievers.

REVELATION 9:7–9

7 And the shapes of the locusts were like unto horses prepared unto battle; and on their heads were as it were crowns like gold, and their faces were as the faces of men.

8 And they had hair as the hair of women, and their teeth were as the teeth of lions.

9 And they had breastplates, as it were breastplates of iron; and the sound of their wings was as the sound of chariots of many horses running to battle.

I know one author who deduced from that passage, "Well, they must be helicopters. That's what a helicopter would sound like." But helicopters don't come out of the bottomless pit. *There aren't any in there!* The Sikorsky Helicopter Company doesn't have a division down there.

Free at Last!

In any case, it's not bombs, hand grenades, helicopters, and implements of war that are coming out of the pit. It's evil spirits that are coming forth. They are described *symbolically* by these details. You can imagine how horrible they must look in the spirit realm. All these things describing them really don't go together. That describes well reprobate beings (vv.7–10).

Remember, these fallen angels have been imprisoned in the pit since the time they fell from the kingdom of heaven. This is the first time they've been loosed on earth like this in great numbers.

King of the Fallen Angels

REVELATION 9:10–11
10 And they had tails like unto scorpions, and there were stings in their tails: and their power was to hurt men five months.
11 And they had a king over them, which is the angel of the bottomless pit, whose name in the Hebrew tongue is Abaddon, but in the Greek tongue hath his name Apollyon.

Both *Abaddon* and *Apollyon* mean "destroyer."

REVELATION 9:12–13
12 One woe is past; and, behold, there come two woes more hereafter.
13 And the sixth angel sounded. . . .

This takes place in the time Jesus referred to as the Great Tribulation. We would do well to remember what He said about it.

MATTHEW 24:22
22 And except those days should be shortened, there should no flesh be saved: but for the elect's sake those days shall be shortened.

Isn't that what Jesus said? No flesh. None. So the days are shortened for the elect's sake. The fallen angels, as we have seen, will not afflict the elect in those days. They will afflict only the ungodly, for that was the command given them.

Loosing the Angels

REVELATION 9:13–14

13 And the sixth angel sounded, and I heard a voice from the four horns of the golden altar which is before God,

14 Saying to the sixth angel which had the trumpet, Loose the four angels which are bound in the great river Euphrates.

The Euphrates River runs through the Middle East. John said four angels are bound in that vicinity. Why would they be bound? Because they're not God's angels. God's angels don't need to be bound, do they? These must be evil angels, fallen angels that have been bound there previously.

We see in scripture that a few fallen angels have been loosed at different seasons. Daniel discovered this when he was praying repentantly to God.

The angel of God came to him and said,

DANIEL 10:12–13

12 . . . Fear not, Daniel: for from the first day that thou didst set thine heart to understand, and to chasten thyself before thy God, thy words were heard, and I am come for thy words.

13 But the prince of the kingdom of Persia withstood me one and twenty days. . . .

"The prince of the kingdom of Persia" the godly angel was referring to was a fallen angel, not the actual ruler of that land. The angel added that after he got through fighting with the prince of Persia, *"Lo, the prince of Grecia* [Greece] *shall come"* (v. 20).

Remember that a few fallen angels are loosed at any given time. Paul refers to them as "spiritual wickedness in high places" (Eph. 6:12).

Here we see four angels that have been bound at the River Euphrates. Your prayers can do that. The prayers of the saints can bind the evil spirits that are loosed in this earth. That is what has bound them in the past, specifically prayer for kings and authorities in that part of the world.

But now evil men are calling upon evil. Now the wicked are doing more wickedly. And that activity in the heavenlies is going to loose what we had bound when we prayed for the peace of that part of the world.

Pray for the Peace of Jerusalem

We in the Body of Christ must continue to "pray for the peace of Jerusalem," or Israel, so that as long as we're in this world, the Jews will experience a certain amount of peace in the Middle East. Even after we're gone, they will have peace to a lesser degree. But later on, evil people will undo that work, and these four evil angels will be loosed.

REVELATION 9:15–16

15 And the four angels were loosed, which were prepared for an hour, and a day, and a month, and a year, for to slay the third part of man.

16 And the number of the army of the horsemen were two hundred thousand thousand: and I heard the number of them.

Two hundred thousand thousand is two hundred million! We know there are that many evil spirits, at the very least, in the spirit realm. This may also correspond to the size of the armies that come to Armageddon in the natural realm.

What these evil spirits are going to stir up in this world is the Battle of Armageddon. They are going to stir up or motivate those who would come to fight Israel. Actually, they're all heading toward that part of the world to join together and fight against God Himself.

And God is going to put an end to it. Jesus is going to return right at the height of the conflict we call Armageddon, and He's going to stop it. And this is how the nations get stirred up to march to Armageddon.

REVELATION 9:17

17 And thus I saw the horses in the vision, and them that sat on them, having breastplates of fire, and of jacinth, and brimstone: and the heads of the horses were as the heads of lions; and out of their mouths issued fire and smoke and brimstone.

A Picture of Warfare

Horses symbolize warfare, of course. This scene describes the spirit beings first, for they have an effect in the natural realm. Then John describes the resulting warfare.

REVELATION 9:18–21

18 By these three was the third part of men killed, by the fire, and by the smoke, and by the brimstone, which issued out of their mouths.

19 For their power is in their mouth, and in their tails: for their tails were like unto serpents, and had heads, and with them they do hurt.

20 And the rest of the men which were not killed by these plagues yet repented not of the works of their hands, that they should not worship devils, and idols of gold, and silver, and brass, and stone, and of wood: which neither can see, nor hear, nor walk:

21 Neither repented they of their murders, nor of their sorceries, nor of their fornication, nor of their thefts.

Chapter 6

The Mystery Is Finished

REVELATION 10:1

1 And I saw another mighty angel come down from heaven, clothed with a cloud: and a rainbow was upon his head, and his face was as it were the sun, and his feet as pillars of fire.

This is a godly angel.

REVELATION 10:2

2 And he had in his hand a little book open: and he set his right foot upon the sea, and his left foot on the earth.

John is talking about the Middle East here. That godly angel is going there with a book that further details the happenings of that time we call the Great Tribulation.

REVELATION 10:3

3 And cried with a loud voice, as when a lion roareth: and when he cried, seven thunders uttered their voices.

Of course, seven is the number that symbolizes fulfillment. In this case, it is the completion of judgment upon the ungodly and those who reject the Gospel, for there will be those who will do that. This little book contains details of that judgment.

REVELATION 10:4

4 And when the seven thunders had uttered their voices, I was about to write: and I heard a voice from heaven saying unto me, Seal up those things which the seven thunders uttered, and write them not.

Why do you suppose God would tell a person something like this? First, armed with this knowledge, we could go to the nearest street corner and tell this to the world. And they wouldn't understand it. Second, they wouldn't receive it.

The Believer's Role

Many people seem to think this withholding of information is to scare the world into the Church. No, it's meant to cause believers to see what happens to the ungodly if they don't come into the Church because only you and I can do something about it beforehand. That's why God wants us to see it. We're the only ones who can change the course of another man's life.

How do we do this? By going to wherever they are and preaching the Gospel to them correctly. John is telling us in great detail what is going to happen to those who reject the truth. But no one *has* to reject the truth. It's their choice.

If you preach and teach with signs and wonders following, you give unsaved people every opportunity to make the right choice. They, the people of the Great Tribulation, are going to have such opportunities under the ministry of the 144,000.

The evil men spoken of in this passage are those who didn't make the right choice. They rejected the truth and received the fulfillment of judgment because of it. Because there is no redeeming effect from this foretaste of the wrath of God being poured out, John doesn't tell us all the details of what is going to happen.

REVELATION 10:5–6

5 And the angel which I saw stand upon the sea and upon the earth lifted up his hand to heaven,

6 And sware by him that liveth for ever and ever, who created heaven, and the things that therein are, and the sea, and the things which are therein, that there should be time no longer.

In other words, we are coming to the point where time as we know it will cease. We will eventually go into eternity.

The Gospel Age Ends

REVELATION 10:7

7 But in the days of the voice of the seventh angel, when he shall begin to sound, the mystery of God should be finished, as he hath declared to his servants the prophets.

This is the last trumpet. This is when the wrath of God will be revealed, and the mystery of God will be finished. What is the mystery? The Age of Grace—the age we're living in—the Gospel Age.

John writes that when the seventh trumpet sounds, the mystery will be finished. T*he preaching of the Gospel will be a completed work.* Those who can respond will have responded, and the wrath of God will now come upon those who have rejected the truth.

REVELATION 10:8

8 And the voice which I heard from heaven spake unto me again, and said, Go and take the little book which is open in the hand of the angel which standeth upon the sea and upon the earth.

The Great Tribulation

The Great Tribulation will be centered in the Middle East. This fact is illustrated by the angel who is standing with his feet upon the sea and upon the earth—upon the nations around Israel and upon Israel herself.

If you throw a rock into a little pond, there is a big splash where the rock hits. Then what happens? Ripples radiate out over the whole pond.

The Great Tribulation is going to be just like that. It's going to be centered in the Middle East, and its greatest effect will be on Israel and its neighbors. However, its ripples will affect all the nations on earth.

Jesus said this Tribulation would be greater than any that went before, and there would never be another that great again. Some people think the Tribulation was already fulfilled in A.D. 70 when Roman legions sacked Jerusalem but that is foolishness.

The massacre and destruction that happened in A.D. 70 was tragic for the Jewish people, but what about the Holocaust they suffered during World War II when 6 million Jews were slaughtered? Would you call that a lesser catastrophe? I wouldn't. Many other great tragedies have happened to the dispersed Jews since then too.

The Great Tribulation hasn't happened yet. It is something that will happen at the close of the age, just like Jesus said it would.

REVELATION 10:8

8 And the voice which I heard from heaven spake unto me again, and said, Go and take the little book which is open in the hand of the angel which standeth upon the sea and upon the earth.

Again, God is letting us know where and when these events will happen.

A Bitter Taste

REVELATION 10:9

9 And I went unto the angel, and said unto him, Give me the little book. And he said unto me, Take it, and eat it up; and it

> shall make thy belly bitter, but it shall be in thy mouth sweet as honey.

Here is something important for us to realize.

REVELATION 10:10–11

10 And I took the little book out of the angel's hand, and ate it up; and it was in my mouth sweet as honey: and as soon as I had eaten it, my belly was bitter.
11 And he said unto me, Thou must prophesy again before many peoples, and nations, and tongues, and kings.

What in the world could this be referring to? You must think about the outer/natural man and the inner/spiritual man for a moment. When men have blasphemed God, rejected all the means by which He has reached out to them, and the only thing that's left for them is judgment—how does God regard it?

God's Point of View

The natural man would say, "They got what was coming to them." That's the *sweetness* in your mouth, but it's a different story to your inner (spiritual) man.

In your spirit, or belly, the death of the wicked should be *bitter.* It's not something to be happy about or gloat over. God sees it as bitterness, and so should we, if we see it correctly in the spirit.

God says in Ezekiel 33:11 that He takes no pleasure in the death of the wicked. In fact, He states this three times in that verse.

A believer should have the same attitude in his heart. He should see it just like God sees it. After all, we are seeing what God made in His own image and likeness being destroyed for lack of faith toward

God. And that's grief. That's tragedy. That's the way the Lord sees it, and that's the way John saw it.

John said, "In my mouth, in my outer man, it seemed like they got what was coming to them. But when I saw in my heart the way God sees, it is bitter. I understood its importance, and it was immediately bitter in my belly."

The contents of that little scroll are the details of the Great Tribulation and the judgment that comes when the wrath of God is poured out at the end of it. And it's bitter to us because God suffers loss whenever any man rejects Him.

The Antichrist Emerges

This thought is continued in the eleventh chapter.

REVELATION 11:1–2

1 And there was given me a reed like unto a rod: and the angel stood, saying, Rise, and measure the temple of God, and the altar, and them that worship therein.

2 But the court which is without the temple leave out, and measure it not; for it is given unto the Gentiles: and the holy city shall they tread under foot forty and two months.

This span of three and a half years is the same period Jesus referred to as the Great Tribulation. The Gentiles will tread over or rule the city of Jerusalem because of the False Prophet misleading the nation of Israel and allying her with the Antichrist.

The Great Tribulation will come upon Israel. Again, it is not going to affect believers as much as unbelievers. It will be a very difficult time for unbelievers. Believers, on the other hand—those who know their God—will do exploits, as the Word says. And the better you know God, the more exploits you'll do. I'm sure that will be just as true in that time/hour as it is today.

Chapter 7

The Two Witnesses

REVELATION 11:3

3 And I will give power unto my two witnesses, and they shall prophesy a thousand two hundred and threescore days, clothed in sackcloth.

God is going to have two witnesses during the Great Tribulation. *Who* they are is not important at all.

People are often trying to identify whether they are Moses, Elijah, Enoch, or someone else from Bible history. They could be Samson and Delilah for all I know. The important thing is that there will be two witnesses. I believe the witnesses will be two anointed, powerful persons God has in that time. I don't really think anyone is going to be resurrected from the past.

In fact, the witnesses could be seen to be *symbolic* of the Word and the Spirit. However, I believe they will also be *literal* men.

Notice God said, *"I will give power unto my two witnesses, and they shall prophesy a thousand two hundred and threescore days."* This is the same period of time that was mentioned in verse 2—three and a half years—the duration of the Great Tribulation.

REVELATION 11:4

4 These are the two olive trees, and the two candlesticks standing before the God of the earth.

Olives produce oil, and oil is a type of the Holy Spirit. The two candlesticks are light bearers. Imagine this right when the Antichrist comes to Jerusalem, proclaims himself to be God, and requires all men on the earth to worship him. Not all of them will. The Antichrist will not have dominion over the whole earth. Some people think he will, but he won't.

It says in Daniel 11:40 that the kings of the north and south will "push at him." Other kings will be in power then who are not necessarily going to be in agreement with him. Although he won't have total control, the Antichrist is going to have a dominating influence over the whole earth.

A Thorn in the Flesh

When he has come to the height of his power—proclaiming that he is going to bring peace to the world (which he never intends to do at all)—these two witnesses will stand right in front of the Antichrist's world headquarters, more or less, and proclaim the truth about him loudly and clearly with a supernatural testimony. And he can't stop them.

Furthermore, the witnesses' testimony against him is going to continue throughout that whole three-and-a half-year period of the Great Tribulation.

REVELATION 11:5

5 And if any man will hurt them, fire proceedeth out of their mouth, and devoureth their enemies. . . .

These witnesses are standing before the god of the earth, challenging his false acts, like the Old Testament prophet Elijah challenged King Ahaziah for seeking after a heathen god (2 Kings 1).

When the backslidden king sent 50 soldiers and their captain to capture the prophet on his mountaintop, fire fell from heaven and consumed them all (v.10).

A company of 50 more soldiers was sent. Again, Elijah called down fire from heaven, and it consumed them as well. The king merely dispatched 50 more with their captain.

How would you like to have been in that third company of 50? They approached the prophet with a different attitude. This third captain fell on his knees and begged, "Have mercy on us, dear prophet," and they were spared (2 Kings 1:13–15). Elijah accompanied them to the palace in Samaria and delivered his rebuke to the king in person (vv. 16–17). The king died.

Leading Candidates

Some people believe one of the two witnesses will be Elijah because he called fire down from heaven in his time. Their usual choice for the second witness is Moses because similar things happened in his life. But it wasn't Elijah or Moses who performed supernatural feats. The Holy Spirit performed the feats through them.

The Bible isn't telling us that Moses, Elijah, Enoch, or anyone else is going to come back to earth to become the two witnesses. The two witnesses will simply be two people who believe God and, as Daniel said, "*The people that do know their God shall be strong, and do exploits*" (Dan. 11:32).

This passage in Revelation chapter 11 about the two witnesses goes on to describe their supernatural powers.

REVELATION 11:5–7

5 . . . and if any man will hurt them, he must in this manner be killed.

6 These have power to shut heaven, that it rain not in the days of their prophecy: and have power over waters to tum them to blood, and to smite the earth with all plagues, as often as they will.

7 And when they shall have finished their testimony, the beast that ascendeth out of the bottomless pit shall make war against them, and shall overcome them, and kill them.

They Die Willingly

This "beast" is a spirit being. It's not so much that he overpowers them. They will lay their lives down voluntarily. I'm sure of that because God never changes His Word. He said, *"These signs shall follow them that believe; In my name shall they shall cast out devils"* (Mark 16:17).

If the devil ever cast out *one* believer, God would have to print "Amendment One" on the Gospel of Mark and add to verse 17, "except on this one day when the devil is going to cast out the believers." Is the devil ever going to be able to cast out believers who *know* their place in Christ? No, he's not, so we can be sure the two believers lay their lives down.

This time, they don't accept the deliverance they have intimately known during the previous three and a half years. They have finished their testimony and have run their course. They have done what God required of them.

REVELATION 11:8–11

8 And their dead bodies shall lie in the street of the great city, which spiritually is called Sodom and Egypt, where also our Lord was crucified.

9 And they of the people and kindreds and tongues and nations
shall see their dead bodies three days and an half, and shall not
suffer their dead bodies to be put in graves.
10 And they that dwell upon the earth shall rejoice over them, and
make merry, and shall send gifts one to another; because these
two prophets tormented them that dwelt on the earth.
11 And after three days and an half the Spirit of life from God
entered into them, and they stood upon their feet; . . .

Resurrected!

They are physically resurrected. I want you to see what the result of this is. Right at the last moment—right at the end of their ministry, there is a great response to the ministry of Christ in them.

Think about that in terms of us, the Gentile Church. While we're here on the earth, it can be the same for us. Wherever there's a testimony of resurrection life, be it spiritual and/or physical, there's always a powerful working of God in the lives of men because of it. Here is an example: Two men who have been dead physically come back to life and stand on their feet!

REVELATION 11:11–12

11 . . . and great fear fell upon them which saw them.
12 And they heard a great voice from heaven saying unto them,
Come up hither. And they ascended up to heaven in a cloud;
and their enemies beheld them.

What happens when their enemies behold all this?

REVELATION 11:13

13 And the same hour was there a great earthquake, and the tenth
part of the city fell, and in the earthquake were slain of men
seven thousand: and the remnant were affrighted, and gave
glory to the God of heaven.

Earthshaking things are happening again spiritually, and an earthquake accompanies them. Notice that even at this last moment, there were people who believed, giving glory to God.

Last-Minute Conversions

Some people, like Thomas, are difficult to persuade. He demanded to see the nail prints and feel the wound on Jesus' side. God could have left Thomas standing there in his unbelief, but God is merciful. What did He do? Jesus came back just for Thomas' sake and said, "All right, Thomas. Quit being unbelieving." And from the testimony of Thomas' life, he started believing then and there.

God knows who will believe, and He will go to *any* length or extreme to reach them. Even at this late hour, having witnessed all they've seen, many haven't yet believed. But God reaches them with this earthshaking happening, the resurrection of His two witnesses.

A Quick Resolution

REVELATION 11:14–15

14 The second woe is past; and, behold, the third woe cometh quickly.

15 And the seventh angel sounded; and there were great voices in heaven, saying, The kingdoms of this world are become the kingdoms of our Lord, and of his Christ. . . .

This part happens quickly because when the wrath of God comes, it comes quickly. The more I study God's Word, the more I believe this conclusion to the Great Tribulation is going to take place in a very short period of time, perhaps in as few as 30 or 45 days.

Although we have studied a number of chapters in detail, we're still not through looking at what happens when the seventh and last trumpet sounds. Time is compressed, and things happen quickly.

Remember, the seventh seal revealed the seven trumpets. Now the seventh trumpet is sounding. What are we going to see? The seven vials that reveal the wrath of God:

REVELATION 11:15–17
15 . . . The kingdoms of this world are become the kingdoms of our Lord, and of his Christ; and he shall reign for ever and ever.
16 And the four and twenty elders, which sat before God on their seats, fell upon their faces, and worshipped God,
17 Saying, We give thee thanks, O Lord God Almighty, which art, and wast, and art to come; because thou hast taken to thee thy great power, and hast reigned.

Jesus' Reign Begins

After the seventh trumpet has sounded, what will happen? Jesus is going to come to reign on the earth.

REVELATION 11:18–19
18 And the nations were angry, and thy wrath is come, and the time of the dead, that they should be judged, and that thou shouldest give reward unto thy servants the prophets, and to the saints, and them that fear thy name, small and great; *and shouldest destroy them which destroy the earth.*
19 And the temple of God was opened in heaven, and there was seen in his temple the ark of his testament: and there were lightnings, and voices, and thunderings, and an earthquake, and great hail.

Here again is a response to those who continue to deny the truth, and you can see why the judgment has to be so severe.

While the saints from the Gentile Church Age are receiving rewards from Jesus in Heaven, the fearful and the unbelieving are receiving judgment and destruction. (It is possible the saints from the Tribulation have also been caught up to God by this time. See Revelation chapters 14 and 15.)

These verses in Revelation chapter 11 are simply more explanation of the events already revealed in Revelation chapters 8, 9, and 10.

The Parenthesis

Revelation 12 is a synopsis, an explanation, a parenthesis of what is happening at this time. All the factors that have caused these events are found in this chapter.

From this information, God is showing us all the things that bear on the age we are living in, and He is helping us realize we are about to enter another age.

You could do the same thing and think about all the things that caused you to be who, what, and where you are today. You would have to go back to the beginning of your life—and even before that to your parents' lives, what happened to your forefathers, and so forth. All these things have a bearing on who, what, and where you are today.

That's what the Lord is doing in Revelation chapter 12. Reading it with this understanding will help you because it is impossible to figure it out in chronological order. I have never been able to make sense out of this chapter in chronological order.

However, if we view chapter 12 as a synopsis of elements from different ages and times, we can understand how they have a bearing on what is happening at the end of this age. A passage in

Revelation chapter 12 bears mightily on Israel in the time of the Great Tribulation.

REVELATION 12:12–17

12 Therefore rejoice, ye heavens, and ye that dwell in them. Woe to the inhabitants of the earth and of the sea! for the devil is come down unto you, having great wrath, because he knoweth that he hath but a short time.

13 And when the dragon saw that he was cast unto the earth, he persecuted the woman which brought forth the man child.

14 And to the woman were given two wings of a great eagle, that she might fly into the wilderness, into her place, where she is nourished for a time, and times, and half a time, from the face of the serpent.

15 And the serpent cast out of his mouth water as a flood after the woman, that he might cause her to be carried away of the flood.

16 And the earth helped the woman, and the earth opened her mouth, and swallowed up the flood which the dragon cast out of his mouth.

17 And the dragon was wroth with the woman, and went to make war with the remnant of her seed, which keep the commandments of God, and have the testimony of Jesus Christ.

In this passage, "earth" and "sea" are symbolic of Israel and her Gentile neighbors, as we have seen before. The devil is referred to as the "dragon" and the "serpent."

The "woman" here symbolizes the believing remnant of God's people—those in a covenant relationship with Him. The "manchild" in verse 13, as well as the second verse of chapter 12, is Jesus Christ.

The "two wings of a great eagle" symbolize the overcoming faith of the woman in times of great testing. "A time, times, and half a time" equals three and a half years. (See Daniel 12:7–11.)

The "flood" cast out of the serpent's mouth (the Antichrist) is persecution aimed at the believing remnant that is soaked up by the unbelieving Jews, or the "earth."

The believers here would have already fled to the place of safety that Jesus told them to flee to in Matthew chapter 24. Frustrated by this, the devil will step up persecution toward the Tribulation saints in the Gentile nations. They are called the "remnant" of the woman's seed in this passage.

Chapter 8

The Beast

We will now go to chapter 13, where John begins by showing us something that happens among the Gentile nations—an empire begins to arise. We are going to see the spirit being that is behind this. Now we are going to see another empire that has been foretold by the prophets, including Daniel.

REVELATION 13:1

1 And I stood upon the sand of the sea, and saw a beast rise up out of the sea. . . .

What does "sea" symbolize? The Gentile nations, especially those in the Eastern Mediterranean region around Israel.

This Greek word for "beast" is different from the word in Revelation chapter 4, which was *zoon. Zoon* means "life," which is usually translated "living creature." Here, the word for "beast" is the Greek word *therion*, which means "poisonous, venomous, dangerous creatures." The creature John saw rise out of the sea is dangerous. This is how John describes it.

REVELATION 13:1

1 . . . having seven heads and ten horns, and upon his horns ten crowns, and upon his heads the name of blasphemy.

The Great Red Dragon

The seven heads and ten horns have to do with Satan's power, as it is described in Revelation 12:3, *"And there appeared another wonder in heaven; and behold a great red dragon, having seven heads and ten horns, and seven crowns upon his heads."*

Here, Satan is typified as the great red dragon. You see his influence over this future kingdom of the Antichrist. Ten earthly kings will reign with the Antichrist, but he is going to reign over them all.

John continues his description.

REVELATION 13:2

2 And the beast which I saw was like unto a *leopard*, and his feet were as the feet of a *bear*, and his mouth as the mouth of *a lion;* and the dragon gave him his power, and his seat, and great authority.

The beast is the Antichrist's empire and Antichrist himself. His authority is given to him by Satan, who has usurped it from men, for the only authority the devil has is what he usurps from men.

REVELATION 13:3

3 And I saw one of his heads as it were wounded to death; and his deadly wound was healed: and all the world wondered after the beast.

We have all speculated about who the Antichrist will be. However, I don't think this symbolizes a person. I think it refers to a nation which is part of Antichrist's empire. More than likely, it is Israel, mortally wounded when the first trumpet sounded and deceived by the False Prophet.

But it is not as important for us to know *which* nation this is as it is for us to understand it is a nation rather than a person. There has been much speculation based on verse 3 that a person will get killed and be brought back to life. I don't think so. It violates God's Word in Hebrews 9:27.

Daniel's Vision

The three creatures of Revelation 13:2 give us a clue as to where the beast will come from. These same three creatures were also referred to by Daniel in a vision he saw.

DANIEL 7:1–6

1 In the first year of Belshazzar king of Babylon Daniel had a dream and visions of his head upon his bed: then he wrote the dream, and told the sum of the matters.
2 Daniel spake and said, I saw in my vision by night, and, behold, the four winds of·the heaven strove upon the great sea.
3 And four great beasts came up from the sea, diverse one from another.
4 The first was like a lion. . . .
5 And behold another beast, a second, like to a bear. . . .
6 After this I beheld, and lo another, like a leopard. . . .

The first creature, the lion, represents the Babylonian Empire, and Daniel uses symbolic terms to tell how the Babylonian Empire came to an end.

The bear symbolizes the empire of the Medes and Persians, the empire that broke through Babylon's defenses and vanquished it in one night. (That was the same night King Belshazzar was terrified by handwriting that supernaturally appeared on a wall during his drunken feast. See Daniel chapter 5.) The Medes and Persians reigned over the region held by the former Babylonian Empire and expanded it somewhat.

Years later, a third earthly king rose to prominence on the world scene. This was Alexander the Great, who came from Macedonia, in Greece. His Greek Empire conquered the Medes and the Persians and expanded their territory even further. After Alexander's death at a young age, his empire was divided into four parts among his four generals. Notice it is predicted in Daniel 7:6 that the leopard had four heads, and dominion was given to it.

The Fourth Beast

The fourth beast—which is seen in Daniel 7:7 coming out of the remnant of the Greek Empire—is representative of the Roman Empire. Many people believe the Antichrist will come from the resurrected *Roman* Empire, but that's not what it says here in Revelation 13:2. We see the empires mentioned form the *Greek* Empire.

Later on, in Daniel 7:19–28, there is mention of a resurrection of the Roman Empire. It indicates that this empire will also give its power and allegiance to the Antichrist.

The Antichrist, however, is coming from the remnant of the Greek Empire, which makes his identity a little more restrictive than it would be if he were coming from a resurrected Roman Empire. It is not a major doctrinal point, but John wants us to know it. From this, I believe we can see that the Antichrist will come from the Middle East.

You will recall that John said in Revelation 13:2, *"And the beast which I saw was like unto a leopard, and his feet were as the feet of a bear."*

Back to Babylon

John is going in reverse order here, backwards from the Greek Empire to the Medo-Persian Empire and beyond.

"And his mouth as the mouth of a Lion" (v. 2). The lion is the Babylonian Empire. The dragon gave him his power, the verse concludes. Then John states in Revelation 13:3 that the head that was wounded to death was healed. The head represents one of the nations in that end-time empire of Antichrist.

REVELATION 13:3–4

3 And I saw one of his heads as it were wounded to death; and his deadly wound was healed: and all the world wondered after the beast.

4 And they worshipped the dragon which gave power unto the beast: and they worshipped the beast, saying, Who is like unto the beast? who is able to make war with him?

So far, we've been looking at the Antichrist's empire and what he's going to rule over. But now the subject shifts to the Antichrist himself; the man who rules that empire.

REVELATION 13:5

5 And there was given unto him a mouth speaking great things and blasphemies; and power was given unto him to continue forty and two months.

That's three and a half years. This verse is really describing the Antichrist himself. During the Great Tribulation, he is going to rule and have influence over his empire and the world for three and a half years.

He will probably have great influence before that period of time too. He is going to proclaim himself to be God and require that men worship him at the beginning of the three and a half years. He is also going to blaspheme God during that three-and-a-half-year period. So the Antichrist, is the mouth speaking...blasphemies.

Who Is "666"?

As we saw in Second Thessalonians chapter 2, the identity of the Antichrist will not be known until the Gentile Church is taken out of the world, for the Gentile Church is the restrainer of the Antichrist. It seems useless for us to speculate about this person's identity. Yet, how many speculations have you heard? I've heard many.

Everyone is trying to figure out who "666" is. To do this, they write out the name of a likely prospect and place a number under each letter of his name. This number usually corresponds to the letter's place in the alphabet. For example, the letter A would be 1, B would be 2, and so forth.

Then they assign other values to these letters, based on some formula they have devised, and eventually they emerge triumphantly with the number 666, "proving" the identity of their candidate for the Antichrist.

During World War II, it should be noted, people "proved" by intricate numerical systems that such infamous dictators as Hitler, Mussolini, and Stalin were *all* "666."

You may argue, "Figures don't lie." No, but liars can still figure. Don't put your faith in numbers. Put your faith in the Word of God. It's the Word that will prove who the Antichrist is.

When the Antichrist Is Revealed

We aren't going to be around when the Antichrist is revealed because the restrainer, the force that restrains him, is the Gentile Church. And Second Thessalonians 2:6–8 says that when the Church is taken out of the way, or raptured, *then* that wicked one will be revealed.

Mankind will not only see *who* he is, they will also see *what* he is. Until you see what he is, you can't really see *who* he is because he is going to appear to be an ordinary ruler—and there are many ordinary rulers in this world.

Suddenly, one of the many people who exercise dominion and authority over parts of the world is going to exalt himself. Satan is going to see to it that this happens, for it is within Satan's dominion to elevate one world ruler over the others if he so desires. And without the Church to restrain him, Satan will enjoy an even greater success in these areas.

You may argue, "Some believers will be alive on the earth then. Why don't they restrain him?"

They will, to a limited extent. For instance, the two witnesses are going to stand before him and proclaim the truth about him to the world. But this will be a different situation. With many brand-new Christians on the scene, most of them won't have much knowledge yet about the believer's authority.

Revival in Israel

We can understand when the Gentile Church is caught away, every saint will go with it, both mature and immature. When that happens, faith will begin in Israel afresh, and large numbers of Jews will repent and receive Jesus as their Messiah. They will be zealous to tell the good news of salvation.

Some—like Stephen and Philip the evangelist in the Early Church—will grow and learn quickly, doing great exploits. Others will learn their position in Christ more slowly and will be more or less run over and pushed aside by the Antichrist.

We have seen such happenings in the present time in Uganda and Cambodia, where the church existed, but it was not grounded and matured in God's Word.

REVELATION 13:6–7

6 And he opened his mouth in blasphemy against God, to blaspheme his name, and his tabernacle, and them that dwell in heaven.

7 And it was given unto him to make war with the saints, and to overcome them: . . .

Permission by Default

Notice, *"it was given unto him."* We saw that phrase before. Who gave this permission to Satan? It comes by Christians not knowing what their dominion is. Yes, some will know their dominion and will do exploits. But the vast majority won't because of the lateness of the hour and the newness of their experience of being born again. They will not be taught in all things yet.

So "it is given" unto Satan to make war with the saints and to overcome them.

REVELATION 13:7–10

7 ...and power was given him over all kindreds, and tongues, and nations.

8 And all that dwell upon the earth shall worship him, whose names are not written in the book of life of the Lamb slain from the foundation of the world.

9 If any man have an ear, let him hear.

10 He that leadeth into captivity shall go into captivity: he that killeth with the sword must be killed with the sword. Here is the patience and the faith of the saints.

In these verses, we again see a fact of that time referred to: the ungodly actively worshiping the Antichrist and Satan. These ungodly are doing more ungodly works. But God reassures the Tribulation saints that these days are limited and full deliverance is theirs by obeying His Word.

Peace, Peace

In verse 11, John tells us, *"And I beheld another beast coming up out of the earth."* Where does this one come from? Out of the earth. This is the one we call the False Prophet. We already saw the effects of what he does in Revelation chapter 8, in the discussion about Wormwood. But here he comes up out of the earth—*out of Israel.*

At a time when everyone is crying out for peace, this man, the False Prophet, is going to appear and make it look like he can lead Israel to peace. Then he is going to lead that nation into a false alliance with the Antichrist.

Verse 11 continues, *"and he has two horns like a lamb."* In other words, he has both *civil* and *religious* authority. He is a person who can lead the nation in both areas. *"And he spake as a dragon."* He speaks the devil's will. He speaks things that put people into bondage!

Great Wonders

REVELATION 13:12–13

12 And he exerciseth all the power of the first beast before him, and causeth the earth and them which dwell therein to worship the first beast, whose deadly wound was healed.

13 And he doeth great wonders, so that he maketh fire come down from heaven on the earth in the sight of men.

The devil can do supernatural signs and wonders through people, so don't be surprised when these things happen. Moses wasn't surprised when he went to Egypt and saw the devil counterfeit supernatural acts through the magicians. He just kept doing what God had told him to do and was vindicated. God's will was accomplished in the Exodus.

The Enemy Is Limited

False or satanic supernatural signs and wonders happen in our day, too, but we are not to be moved by them. Just keep on doing what God has told you to do. Know that there is a limit to what the enemy can do. *Satan's power is not unlimited. God's power is.* Remember, Satan came to the end of his power in Egypt, didn't he?

Whatever Moses did, the magicians copied until the day God said to Moses,

EXODUS 8:16

16 . . . Say unto Aaron, Stretch out thy rod, and smite the dust of the land, that it may become lice throughout all the land of Egypt.

Until then, the magicians had been able to duplicate Moses' supernatural signs. They, too, had brought forth frogs and turned water into blood. Now Aaron cast his rod upon the sand and *"all the dust of the land became lice throughout all the land of Egypt"* (v.17).

Once again, the magicians sought to do the same with their enchantments. If you can bring forth frogs, you ought to be able to make lice, but they couldn't. The enemy's power came to an end in Egypt that day.

Although Satan has great power and exercises it through people who give him authority to do so, there is an end to his power. His is not an unlimited power. That is the point you need to understand here.

Greater Power

God's people have greater power, if they only knew it. Some don't seem to know it. During the time of the False Prophet in Israel, many won't know their authority because of the newness of their Christian experience. The same thing happens today. New believers often get "run over" by the devil.

It will be difficult for people to get saved in the time of the Great Tribulation, but they can if they believe God's Word. I wouldn't recommend waiting until then, though.

The False Prophet is going to deceive the people of the earth, and he is going to perform satanic wonders.

REVELATION 13:14
14 And deceiveth them that dwell on the earth by the means of those miracles. . . .

Many people in the present hour are deceived by this very thing, for satanic wonders are in evidence today.

REVELATION 13:14–15
14 . . . which he had power to do in the sight of the beast; saying to them that dwell on the earth, that they should make an image to the beast, which had the wound by a sword, and did live.
15 And he had power to give life unto the image of the beast, that the image of the beast should both speak, and cause that as many as would not worship the image of the beast should be killed.

There is an agreement with the Antichrist through this False Prophet that will put him in dominion over the nation of Israel. And there will be a literal image like Nebuchadnezzar raised up that everyone is required to worship. Nebuchadnezzar really wanted the people to worship *him*, and the image reflected that.

The Mark of the Beast

REVELATION 13:16

16 And he causeth all, both small and great, rich and poor, free and bond, to receive a mark in their right hand, or in their foreheads.

I've heard this taught as if members of the Gentile Church will have to decide whether to receive the mark of the beast. No, they won't. They're not going to be around at that time.

It is those who have come to faith in the time of the Great Tribulation who will face this problem. Will these believers receive the mark? No, I don't think so. Will nonbelievers receive it? Yes, I believe they will.

How will men know the difference? Think of the commonly repeated truth that water baptism is an *outward* sign of an *inward* work of grace. Baptism to you and me is an outward sign of something that has happened to us inwardly.

Likewise, this mark of the beast is something men who follow the ways of the Antichrist will take during the Great Tribulation because they have hardened themselves and rejected God. They follow the Antichrist inwardly and trust in his satanic acts rather than in God.

The more supernatural power the Church exhibits on earth, the more supernatural acts the devil will have to manufacture to lure people away, twisting their thinking.

Blasphemy

Followers of the Antichrist will call good "evil" and evil "good." For example, when the Holy Spirit is in manifestation, they will call that "evil." That's blasphemy against the Holy Spirit. Jesus taught about it in Matthew 12:22–32. But when familiar spirits operate, they will call that "good."

These people have blasphemed everything God has in His power to show them the truth. There is nothing else God can do for them. What else could He do to show them the truth?

Although the nation of Israel will fall into the Antichrist's orbit and will be controlled by what he does, some people in the nation will escape.

Jesus spoke to these who will believe in Matthew chapter 24, when He said,

MATTHEW 24:15–16

15 When ye therefore shall see the abomination of desolation, spoken of by Daniel the prophet, stand in the holy place, (whoso readeth, let him understand:)

16 Then let them which be in Judaea flee into the mountains.

A Place of Safety

A place of safety is prepared and awaiting these Jewish believers to flee to. It is on or near their border, a place the Antichrist will not have dominion and control over. It probably includes the ancient desert city of Petra in the nation of Jordan because its location is described by the names of the peoples who lived there, Edom, Moab, and Ammon (Dan. 11:41).

Who would know to go to this refuge except those who had read the New Testament? It isn't mentioned in the Old Testament. And how many Jews know the New Testament that well? Only the ones who have been saved would know to flee. Jesus said to these who will be kept from that Great Tribulation, "Flee! Get out of there!"

These are some of the conditions they will be fleeing from.

REVELATION 13:16–18

16 And he causeth all . . . to receive a mark in their right hand, or in their foreheads:
17 And that no man might buy or sell, save he that had the mark, or the name of the beast, or the number of his name.
18 Here is wisdom. Let him that hath understanding count the number of the beast: for it is a number of a man; and his number is Six hundred threescore and six.

The number 666 symbolizes man and his work, but 777 symbolizes God and His work. When I met my wife, June, her address was 777 El Camino Real (the King's Highway), Apartment 7. I told her, "You must be a good person." It's a good thing she didn't live down the street at 666!

Some people try to be guided by numerology. Little merit is in it, so don't go overboard with it. Don't try to apply it to every little thing you think and do in your life. Use numerology only if it obviously and definitely applies to a situation.

The End of the Line for Ungodly Men

The Antichrist is the fulfillment of man's effort without God!

The Antichrist represents man trying to do his own thing. And this is the end of it—a man who is totally possessed and controlled by the devil. And this man is *trying* to control the rest of the earth the same way, but he will never really succeed.

Although the Antichrist will have a great influence on all the earth, he won't totally dominate it. The number 666 represents him, his work, and that which is given over by man to the devil to dominate.

No "Ultimate Reconciliation"

Not everyone is going to be saved—no matter what anyone says. The Bible definitely teaches there are those who won't come to the faith.

Every few years, however, the "ultimate reconciliation" error comes around again. Fifteen years ago, it was especially strong, but I haven't heard much about it lately.

Those who hold this position believe God is going to win everyone sooner or later. They agree that people who didn't repent before dying will have to go into the Lake of Fire. But they say after these sinners have been there a thousand years, they're going to repent.

There's more to repentance than just being sorry. People can be sorry but not repent, for *natural* sorrow doesn't necessarily mean repentance. If sinners didn't repent before death, they're not going to repent afterward. *Godly sorrow is repentance.* True repentance changes the way you act.

Judas was *sorry* for what he had done, but he didn't *repent.* He was just sorry his scheme didn't work because there were consequences he didn't like. He would have done the same thing again. That is why his natural grief overcame him and led him to suicide.

Caught Away With the Lamb

We need to turn our attention to some significant events in chapter 14:

REVELATION 14:1

1 I looked, and lo, a Lamb stood on the mount Sion, and with him an hundred forty and four thousand. . . .

The 144,000 Jewish believers have finished their ministry by this time, and they, too, have been caught away with the Lord. This is one of the other catchings away found in scripture.

Some people see this reference and think it refers to the Gentile Church, but it refers to the 144,000 and the fruit of their ministry being caught away. They're seen here with the Lamb.

Back in chapter 7, we saw the fruit of their ministry out of all the nations of the earth, every nation, every tribe, every tongue, and every kindred.

Mystery Babylon

One of the next things that happens is revealed.

REVELATION 14:8

8 And there followed another angel, saying, Babylon is fallen, is fallen, that great city, because she made all nations drink of the wine of the wrath of her fornication.

What is Babylon? Mystery Babylon referred to here and in Revelation chapters 16 through 19 is *this present world system* of commerce, materialism, politics, religion, and power that Satan manipulates to keep men deceived and separated from God the Father.

This system will be totally destroyed after all who will respond to the Gospel of Jesus Christ have done so and have come out of that world system and the kingdom of darkness and have been born into the kingdom of heaven.

The record of that destruction and the wrath of Almighty God is clearly recorded in chapters 16 through 19. Without going into a verse-by-verse exposition of these chapters, we can summarize by saying that death and destruction come to those nations and all men who have hardened themselves time after time against God and all He has done to reach them with the truth of Jesus Christ.

When God's wrath is poured out upon all that has become reprobate, it will be completely destroyed. This includes Mystery Babylon. It shall be no more. During the Millennium, Jesus will reign with His saints, and the only system on earth will be His glorious kingdom. Hallelujah!

Chapter 9

The Lord God Omnipotent Reigneth

We will now move ahead to study chapter 19.

REVELATION 19:1–6

1 And after these things I heard a great voice of much people in heaven, saying, Alleluia; Salvation, and glory, and honour, and power, unto the Lord our God.

2 For true and righteous are his judgments: for he hath judged the great whore, which did corrupt the earth with her fornication, and hath avenged the blood of his servants at her hand.

3 And again they said, Alleluia. And her smoke rose up for ever and ever.

4 And the four and twenty elders and the four beasts fell down and worshipped God that sat on the throne, saying, Amen; Alleluia.

5 And a voice came out of the throne, saying, Praise our God, all ye his servants, and ye that fear him, both small and great.

6 And I heard as it were the voice of a great multitude, and as the voice of many waters, and as the voice of mighty thunderings, saying, Alleluia: for the Lord God omnipotent reigneth.

This great multitude, described here as *"the voice of many waters,"* represents the saved from all ages. The Old Covenant saints, the saints from the Gentile Church Age, the Tribulation saints—all who have believed on the Lord Jesus Christ—are seen here. This is truly "spiritual Israel," ready to return to earth with Christ and reign forever with Him.

The Church in Heaven

Notice verse 1, where John writes, *"I heard a great voice of much people in heaven."* Where were the people? In Heaven. Yet, some say the Church isn't going to Heaven. She is just going to meet Jesus in the air and return to earth again. But this says the saved are in Heaven.

We see more about the Bride of Christ.

REVELATION 19:7–8

7 Let us be glad and rejoice, and give honour to him: for the marriage of the Lamb is come, and his wife hath made herself ready.
8 And to her was granted that she should be arrayed in fine linen, clean and white: for the fine linen is the righteousness of saints.

Your Two Garments

I want you to see something. You, the saints of God, are already clothed in righteousness. You have a white garment of righteousness that Jesus gave you at your New Birth. The white linen garment mentioned in verse 8 goes beyond that garment, however. It is a wedding garment.

John said in verse 7, *"his wife hath made herself ready."* You don't make yourself ready for salvation, do you? Is there anything you can do to make yourself saved? No. In fact, verse 8 says, *"She should be arrayed in fine linen, clean and white: for the fine linen is the righteousness of saints."*

If you look at other translations, almost everyone will render "righteousness" as "the righteous acts" or "the upright deeds." In other words, works that proceed from faith, hope, and love—works sown to the spirit.

It is these things that make the Bride of Christ ready. It is these things that will qualify the Bride, the Body, to be totally united with Her Head, the Bridegroom, Jesus Christ.

This is pointing out that it is not by works of the flesh that the Bride will be made ready—absolutely not. It is works of righteousness that come from being in right standing with God that the Bride will make herself ready by being obedient to her Head.

The Marriage Supper

John continues.

REVELATION 19:9–10

9 And he saith unto me, Write, Blessed are they which are called unto the marriage supper of the Lamb. And he saith unto me, These are the true sayings of God.

10 And I fell at his feet to worship him. And he said unto me, See thou do it not: I am thy fellowservant, and of thy brethren that have the testimony of Jesus: worship God: for the testimony of Jesus is the spirit of prophecy.

What is the spirit of prophecy? The testimony of Jesus, not the testimony of the Antichrist, the False Prophet, the Great Tribulation, or anything else.

As we look over these truths from Revelation, we need to remember that grace and peace are being communicated to us. We know what's going to happen. We know God has a plan that will be fulfilled, and the Church *will* succeed.

The fact the Church hasn't seemed to succeed for a long time does not prove that she won't. She will. God said so. He knows we will succeed, and He knows when we will succeed. This generation can see the truth, the will, and the plan of God in many different lights.

The Rod of Iron

REVELATION 19:11–16

11 And I saw heaven opened, and behold a white horse; and he that sat upon him was called Faithful and True, and in righteousness he doth judge and make war.

12 His eyes were as a flame of fire, and on his head were many crowns; and he had a name written, that no man knew, but he himself.

13 And he was clothed with a vesture dipped in blood: and his name is called The Word of God.

14 And the armies which were in heaven followed him upon white horses, clothed in fine linen, white and clean.

15 And out of his mouth goeth a sharp sword, that with it he should smite the nations: and he shall rule them with a rod of iron; and he treadeth the winepress of the fierceness and wrath of Almighty God.

16 And he hath on his vesture and on his thigh a name written, KING OF KINGS, AND LORD OF LORDS.

Christ is going to take His power to Himself and reign over the kingdoms of this world. We have seen references to this in chapter 11 and other passages, but here we see it pictured in detail. Like Enoch prophesied, *"Behold, the Lord cometh with ten thousands of his saints"* (Jude 14).

John Sees Armageddon

John saw further into the end of time: He saw what happens to the beast and the False Prophet when judgment falls on them. John saw Armageddon.

REVELATION 19:19–21

19 And I saw the beast, and the kings of the earth, and their armies, gathered together to make war against him that sat on the horse, and against his army.

20 And the beast was taken, and with him the false prophet that wrought miracles before him, with which he deceived them that had received the mark of the beast, and them that worshipped his image. These both were cast alive into a lake of fire burning with brimstone.

21 And the remnant were slain with the sword of him that sat upon the horse, which sword proceeded out of his mouth: and all the fowls were filled with their flesh.

Chapter 10

The Millennial Kingdom

In chapter 20, John saw the point at which we go into the next dispensation, the thousand-year period we call the Millennium.

REVELATION 20:1–3

1 And I saw an angel come down from heaven, having the key of the bottomless pit and a great chain in his hand.
2 And he laid hold on the dragon, that old serpent, which is the Devil, and Satan, and bound him a thousand years,
3 And cast him into the bottomless pit, and shut him up, and set a seal upon him, that he should deceive the nations no more, till the thousand years should be fulfilled: and after that he must be loosed a season.

The fact that an angel possesses the key to the bottomless pit proves that the place is controlled by the Lord. All Satan's demons and fallen angels will accompany him to the pit.

The Millennium Begins

REVELATION 20:4–5

4 And I saw thrones, and they sat upon them, and judgment was given unto them: and I saw the souls of them that were beheaded for the witness of Jesus, and for the word of God, and which had not worshipped the beast, neither his image, neither had received his mark upon their foreheads, or in their hands; and they lived and reigned with Christ a thousand years.
5 But the rest of the dead lived not again until the thousand years were finished. This is the first resurrection.

Who is resurrected in the first resurrection? The *righteous.* Who is resurrected in the second? The *unrighteous.* They appear before the Great White Throne, which is also mentioned in this chapter.

Satan on the Loose

REVELATION 20:7–8

7 And when the thousand years are expired, Satan shall be loosed out of his prison.

8 And shall go out to deceive the nations which are in the four quarters of the earth, Gog and Magog, to gather them together to battle: the number of whom is as the sand of the sea.

The earth will be repopulated by natural men, not the glorified saints, in the Millennium. Satan is not going out to deceive the glorified saints because glorified saints can't be deceived, and Satan will have no access to them. Also, there is neither unrenewed mind nor unglorified flesh in the glorified saints.

Therefore, Satan's target will be the natural people who have repopulated the earth. These natural men could come from children below the age of accountability who pass from the Age of Grace into the Millennium.

The "sand of the sea" is symbolic of these natural men. Satan will deceive some of mankind and gather an army out of the nations to come and fight God one last time.

REVELATION 20:9

9 And they went up on the breadth of the earth, and compassed the camp of the saints about, and the beloved city: and fire came down from God out of heaven, and devoured them.

There wasn't any battle—just an immediate judgment on what they were doing. That is a characteristic of the Millennial Kingdom.

Youngsters at 100

Men will have seen the Word of God and will have had the opportunity to believe it. It says in Isaiah 65:20 that natural human beings who will die at one hundred years of age will be thought to be accursed.

People are going to live throughout the entire Millennial reign. But they aren't going to have the same lifespan people have now. All this has to do with the curse being lifted from the earth.

ISAIAH 65:17–25

17 For, behold, I create new heavens and a new earth: and the former shall not be remembered, nor come into mind.

18 But be ye glad and rejoice for ever in that which I create: for, behold, I create Jerusalem a rejoicing, and her people a joy.

19 And I will rejoice in Jerusalem, and joy in my people: and the voice of weeping shall be no more heard in her, nor the voice of crying.

20 There shall be no more thence an infant of days, nor an old man that hath not filled his days: for the child shall die an hundred years old; but the sinner being an hundred years old shall be accursed.

21 And they shall build houses, and inhabit them; and they shall plant vineyards, and eat the fruit of them.

22 They shall not build, and another inhabit; they shall not plant, and another eat: for as the days of a tree are the days of my people, and mine elect shall long enjoy the work of their hands.

23 They shall not labour in vain, nor bring forth for trouble; for they are the seed of the blessed of the Lord, and their offspring with them.

24 And it shall come to pass, that before they call, I will answer; and
while they are yet speaking, I will hear.
25 The wolf and the lamb shall feed together, and the lion shall
eat straw like the bullock: and dust shall be the serpent's
meat. They shall not hurt nor destroy in all my holy moun-
tain, saith the Lord.

When judgment comes to these people, it will be because they have rejected the truth that has filled the earth (Isaiah 11:9) and which they have had so long to receive. Some of them will be deceived by Satan, and some will not.

Those who are deceived will reject God when they are tested and tempted. They will rebel and follow the devil in the short time he has, which is cut short by the judgment of fire from Heaven.

Cast Into the Lake of Fire

REVELATION 20:10

10 And the devil that deceived them was cast into the lake of fire and brimstone, where the beast and the false prophet are, and shall be tormented day and night for ever and ever.

The latter have been in the lake of fire during the entire Millennium, haven't they? Satan himself now joins them in what has become his final destination.

Separated From God Forever

Man has a choice. God will not override anyone's will—not now and not ever. When men turn away from all the means God has used to reach out to them and reject what God has done in sending His Son as a sacrifice, they will ultimately be separated from God forever.

God tells us to preach the Gospel to everyone. We have no way of knowing who will accept it and who will reject it. Some men and women we think are the most unlikely candidates surprise us by turning from their wicked ways and receiving the truth.

I've seen God reach down to people who were in the depths of alcoholism or some other bondage and yank them out of it when they cried out to Him. He can do it.

The Final Judgment

Let's look at the Great White Throne—the final judgment. All judgment that agrees with the Word of God purifies or separates the holy from the unholy. We believers do that for ourselves during this lifetime as we judge ourselves by the Word of God (1 Cor. 11:31).

At some point in the future, God will separate everyone who has rejected Him from everyone who has been united with Him, and the two will never meet again. And we will find that nothing like this will ever happen again.

REVELATION 20:11–12

11 And I saw a great white throne, and him that sat on it, from whose face the earth and the heaven fled away; and there was found no place for them.

12 And I saw the dead, small and great, stand before God; and the books were opened: and another book was opened, which is the book of life: and the dead were judged out of those things which were written in the books, according to their works.

No Believers There

No believers are going to stand at the Great White Throne. The unrighteous dead are judged at this time. This judgment is for unbelievers—those who have been unrighteous and have rejected Jesus Christ. God is just. He will show them the sinful things they did.

REVELATION 20:13-15

13 And the sea gave up the dead which were in it; and death and hell delivered up the dead which were in them: and they were judged every man according to their works.
14 And death and hell were cast into the lake of fire. This is the second death.
15 And whosoever was not found written in the book of life was cast into the lake of fire.

This is the second death. There is no appeal from spiritual death once you are dead.

As long as you live in this world, you can choose to receive eternal life by accepting Jesus. Even though you are spiritually dead and are living separated from God, you can be made spiritually alive and enjoy eternal life now and in the world to come. However, once you have died, there is no way to come back and receive Jesus. There is no appeal from the second death.

Our Glorious Future

John describes the glorious future that lies ahead for the redeemed.

REVELATION 21:1

1 And I saw a new heaven and a new earth: for the first heaven and the first earth were passed away; and there was no more sea.

Although some may think this means there will be no more ocean, I feel sure it means there will be no more heathen. There are no people left who do not believe in God. The unbelievers have been totally and eternally separated from God and His kingdom.

REVELATION 21:2

2 And I John saw the holy city, new Jerusalem, coming down from God out of heaven, prepared as a bride adorned for her husband.

A city is where people live. Jesus is the Cornerstone of that city, and you're a part of it, too, as a lively stone. Do you remember you are called "lively stones" in First Peter 2:5?

Some people teach the Bride is not the saints. They say the Bride is a city. No, the saints are definitely the Bride, because a city without its people is no city at all.

No Tears, No Death, No Sorrow, No Pain

REVELATION 21:3–4

3 And I heard a great voice out of heaven saying, Behold the tabernacle of God is with men, and he will dwell with them, and they shall be his people, and God himself shall be with them, and be their God.

4 And God shall wipe away all tears from their eyes; and there shall be no more death, neither sorrow, nor crying, neither shall there be any more pain: for the former things are passed away.

We will not go through eternity hampered by any regrets. Look at this, *"God shall wipe away all tears from their eyes."* Hallelujah!

Nothing is ever going to die again. That means you aren't going to dine on T-bone steak in Heaven because that cow isn't going to die to give it to you. (I'm sure God has something better than steak!) *"There shall be no more death."*

There will be nothing to be sorrowful about. There will be nothing to cry about. *"Neither shall there be any more pain."* The tip of your little finger will never bother you again. Nothing will ever hurt you again. Imagine that. *"For the former things are passed away."* They're gone forever, never to return.

Seeing Face to Face

REVELATION 21:5–6

5 And he that sat upon the throne said, Behold, I make all things new. And he said unto me, Write: for these words are true and faithful.

6 And he said unto me, It is done. I am Alpha and Omega, the beginning and the end. I will give unto him that is athirst of the fountain of the water of life freely.

Paul said, *"For now we see through a glass, darkly; but then face to face: now I know in part; but then shall I know even as also I am known"* (1 Cor. 13:12).

I don't think we'll ever know everything there is to know about God because He is an infinite being. In eternity, we are always going to be learning something wonderful and new about Him.

We will no longer be hampered by hindrances to our understanding. We face a number of hindrances today to complete understanding. The first and greatest is the fact that we have to contend with our flesh. In Heaven, we aren't going to be hindered by flesh. It will not be mortal but immortal. Not corruptible but incorruptible.

Second, the devil tries to hinder us at every turn. When we reach Heaven, he isn't going to be around. Third, there will no longer be a world system trying to separate us from God. With nothing to hinder us, we will be free to know everything we want to.

God's at Work on Planet Earth

Another important verse follows.

REVELATION 21:7

7 He that overcometh shall inherit all things; and I will be his God, and he shall be my son.

Everything God made, He made for you. Think about that. God is working in one little corner of the universe called planet Earth. What a tiny place earth is. Go out and look at the stars some night and consider what a tiny planet we inhabit in the vast universe.

In 1990, the Voyager 1 spacecraft sent back a photograph from the edge of our galaxy that shows planet Earth as "a little blue dot" in the vast sea of space. Scientists, deeply moved, promptly dubbed it "The Photograph of the Century."

It's on planet Earth that God is perfecting life. He's doing it here. He's bringing all things into perfection here. God doesn't tell us all the details, because He doesn't want us to get so interested in the details of eternity that we lose sight of the tasks He has given us to perform in this life.

Visions of Heaven

All the people who have ever had a vision of Heaven said the same thing. They didn't want to return to earth. You can't blame them after all the wonders they saw and experienced.

In speaking of his own experience, Paul said it was unlawful to talk about those things. What he meant was there was no way he could describe what he saw in Heaven.

Visions of Heaven often share similar characteristics. After a person is shown a portion of Heaven, God may then show him the mass of suffering, dying humanity that inhabits our globe. Next, he may be granted a terrifying glimpse into hell itself, so he will understand what conditions are like there.

When it is time for the person to return to earth, God will exhort him, "Remember what you saw. That's why you have to go back." Otherwise, no one would ever want to return to earth.

Torn Between Heaven and Earth

What if God revealed everything about Heaven to us now? We would be like the people who have had a vision of Heaven. Even though we were on earth, we would *long* to be over there, enjoying Heaven's total perfection. We might even lose our will to live.

But God has a purpose for our being here, and we need to fulfill it. We need to "finish our course," like the Apostle Paul did.

God is perfecting life here on planet Earth. He did not fill up the whole universe with life. Some people think there is life on other planets. The Bible doesn't say a word about it. If life is out there, God hasn't said anything about it yet.

There's Life on One Planet

The Bible mentions only two places in the universe where life exists: Heaven and earth. When various stars or planets are mentioned in scripture, life is not mentioned as being there.

I think I understand why this would be. In Isaiah 1:18, God invited us to reason with Him, so let's reason a little with the Word of God.

God is not willing to suffer the enormous loss of His creation. He would not have filled up the whole universe with life, just to watch it all turn out badly and lose it all.

What God is doing now is perfecting life here on earth. Once it is perfected, what is He going to do with it? What are all of those stars and planets out there for—for sailors to navigate by? I think God has a greater design than that for His universe. I don't think He hung all those stars up there for nothing.

Filling the Universe With Life

I believe God is going to fill the universe with that perfected life. And you're a part of that life. You're going to enjoy life for eternity with God. *"He that overcometh shall inherit all things."* Whatever God has made—whatever is eternally perfect—is yours. You inherit it.

REVELATION 21:8–12

8 But the fearful, and unbelieving, and the abominable, and murderers, and whoremongers, and sorcerers, and idolaters, and all liars, shall have their part in the lake which burneth with fire and brimstone: which is the second death.

9 And there came unto me one of the seven angels which had the seven vials full of the seven last plagues, and talked with me, saying, Come hither, I will shew thee the bride, the Lamb's wife.

10 And he carried me away in the spirit to a great and high mountain, and shewed me that great city, the holy Jerusalem, descending out of heaven from God.

11 Having the glory of God: and her light was like unto a stone most precious, even like a jasper stone, clear as crystal;

12 And had a wall great and high, and had twelve gates, and at the gates twelve angels, and names written thereon, which are the names of the twelve tribes of the children of Israel.

Chapter 11

✡

The Eternal Kingdom

We are looking here at the eternal kingdom, God's dazzling city, descending out of heaven, clothed with His glory. That other kingdom we've had on earth, Mystery Babylon, has been destroyed.

All things on earth will now be governed by Jesus Christ in and through God's city.

John continues his wondrous vision.

REVELATION 21:22–27

22 And I saw no temple therein: for the Lord God Almighty and the Lamb are the temple of it.

23 And the city had no need of the sun, neither of the moon, to shine in it: for the glory of God did lighten it, and the Lamb is the light thereof.

24 And the nations of them which are saved shall walk in the light of it: and the kings of the earth do bring their glory and honour into it.

25 And the gates of it shall not be shut at all by day: for there shall be no night there.

26 And they shall bring the glory and honour of the nations into it.

27 And there shall in no wise enter into it anything that defileth, neither whatsoever worketh abomination, or maketh a lie: but they which are written in the Lamb's book of life.

This does not mean that all the liars and other sinners are going to be camped outside the city gates. By this time, sadly, they are already eternally separated from God. There is not even going to be any remembrance of them, for God shall wipe away all tears from the saints' eyes.

No More Curse

REVELATION 22:1–3

1 And he shewed me a pure river of water of life, clear as crystal, proceeding out of the throne of God and of the Lamb.

2 In the midst of the street of it, and on either side of the river, was there the tree of life, which bare twelve manner of fruits, and yielded her fruit every month: and the leaves of the tree were for the healing of the nations.

3 And there shall be no more curse: . . .

If you think about it, why was there a curse in the first place? What did God curse? Sin and disobedience. And how was the curse lifted—how was the debt paid? By the blood Jesus Christ spilled on the cross.

The blood of Jesus Christ is bringing all things into perfection. What will this accomplish? In eternity, there will never be another failure. There will never be another being who will do what Lucifer did.

As you know, God created Lucifer as a great, mighty, powerful spirit being, but he rebelled against God, and God cursed that rebellion.

When God recreated the earth and created Adam and Eve, they fell. God cursed their rebellion too. (See Genesis chapters 1–3.)

There will be no more curse in eternity, for there will be no more rebellion. It's simply not going to happen. There is nothing in all eternity that will ever again rebel against God or get out of His will.

The Keeping Power of the Blood

In eternity, all creation will have been brought into God's will and will be kept there by the blood of the Lord Jesus. If you know that, you know your position in Christ Jesus. You're in Him, and Jesus' blood will keep you, just like God said it would (Phil. 1:6).

In the Eternal Kingdom, there will be no more crying, no more sorrow, no more pain, no more curse—nothing that needs to be cursed.

REVELATION 22:3–5

3 . . . but the throne of God and of the Lamb shall be in it; and his servants shall serve him:

4 And they shall see his face; and his name shall be in their foreheads.

5 And there shall be no night there; and they need no candle, neither light of the sun; for the Lord God giveth them light: and they shall reign for ever and ever.

They shall reign with God forever and ever as kings and priests unto Him. Forever and ever—without limit. This is the same term that describes what will happen to sinners throughout all eternity. They will be separated from God forever and ever.

No New Revelation

REVELATION 22:6–7

6 And he said unto me, These sayings are faithful and true: and the Lord God of the holy prophets sent his angel to shew unto his servants the things which must shortly be done.

7 Behold, I come quickly: blessed is he that keepeth the sayings of the prophecy of this book.

This is not a new revelation. It is the same revelation you've heard over and over again. Jesus first taught it in the Book of Matthew.

MATTHEW 7:24

24 Therefore whosoever heareth these sayings of mine, and doeth them, I will liken him unto a wise man, which built his house upon a rock.

As you already know, you're blessed if you hear and do the words of the Lord Jesus.

Completed in Christ

REVELATION 22:8–11

8 And I John saw these things, and heard them. And when I had heard and seen, I fell down to worship before the feet of the angel which shewed me these things.

9 Then saith he unto me, See thou do it not: for I am thy fellowservant, and of thy brethren the prophets, and of them which keep the sayings of this book: worship God.

10 And he saith unto me, Seal not the sayings of the prophecy of this book: for the time is at hand.

11 He that is unjust, let him be unjust still: and he which is filthy, let him be filthy still: and he that is righteous, let him be righteous still: and he that is holy, let him be holy still.

As we saw above, all things will remain the way they are completed in Christ. After the Great White Throne Judgment, nothing that is righteous will ever be unrighteous. And those who have been separated from God because they rejected Him will never be seen or heard from again.

John then quotes the thrilling words he heard Jesus speak.

REVELATION 22:12–13
12 And, behold, I come quickly; and my reward is with me, to give every man according as his work shall be.
13 I am Alpha and Omega, the beginning and the end, the first and the last.

God has no beginning and no ending but this age does. It was in this age that God began a work with man, starting with the creation of Adam and ending with the Great White Throne. From this time forward, man will be perfected with God forever.

Jesus Rewards Faithfulness

Notice in verse 12 that the Lord will reward you according to what you have done in this lifetime. He will particularly reward you for faithfulness. We know this from what Jesus said to both of the hard-working servants in the Parable of the Talents:

MATTHEW 25:21
21 . . . Well done, thou good and *faithful* servant: thou hast been faithful over a few things, I will make thee ruler over many things: enter thou into the joy of thy lord.

In this parable, the master had given one servant five talents and the other two talents. Each doubled his sum of money. Although the number of talents they had been given differed, notice their reward was the same.

The reward is the same for faithfulness, whether you work in a large ministry, reaching millions, or you minister to one person at a time. If you're doing what God told you to do, the reward for your faithfulness will be exactly the same.

It is vital that we see God's purposes in whatever we do and not look at what other people are doing and think we should be imitating them. Listen to God, and do what He tells you to do. That is faithfulness.

The Fruit of Faithfulness

God's faithfulness is reproduced in believers, for faithfulness is a fruit of the spirit. The *King James Version* translates Galatians 5:22 as *"The fruit of the Spirit is love, joy, peace, longsuffering, gentleness, goodness, faith."*

Most other translations translate the word "faith" as "faithfulness." The fruit of the spirit is faithfulness. That's what God has reproduced in us. We have His nature, His ability, and His character. And as His character grows in us, we develop and become more faithful day by day.

When Jesus says, "Well done, thou good and faithful servant," He's talking to you. He's talking to those who are faithful.

You have a part to play in your ministry by being faithful. Paul taught, *"Make full proof of thy ministry"* (2 Tim. 4:5). *"Stir up the gift of God, which is in thee"* (2 Tim. 1:6). Use your ministry gift at every opportunity. Do that which God has shown you to do. When you do, you'll find God has a reward for you. God rewards those who are faithful.

REVELATION 22:14–15

14 Blessed are they that do his commandments, that they may have right to the tree of life, and may enter in through the gates into the city.

15 For without are dogs and sorcerers, and whoremongers, and murderers, and idolaters, and whosoever loveth and maketh a lie.

Again, these wicked people are not camped outside God's city. They are eternally separated from God and the saints.

We Shall Be As He Is

REVELATION 22:16

16 I Jesus have sent mine angel to testify unto you these things in the churches. I am the root and the offspring of David, and the bright and morning star.

What did Jesus say back in the second chapter?

REVELATION 2:26, 28

26 And he that overcometh, and keepeth my works unto the end, to him will I give . . .

28 . . . the morning star.

Jesus is going to give you the same thing He is—eternal life. The full ability to be enlightening.

We will be eternal creatures who will be enlightening one to another. We will be overcomers during our journey through this world until we live fully in God's Eternal Kingdom.

REVELATION 22:17–19

17 And the Spirit and the bride say, Come. And let him that heareth say, Come. And let him that is athirst come. And whosoever will, let him take the water of life freely.

18 For I testify unto every man that heareth the words of the prophecy of this book, If any man shall add unto these things, God shall add unto him the plagues that are written in this book:

19 And if any man shall take away from the words of the book of this prophecy, God shall take away his part out of the book

of life, and out of the holy city, and from the things which are written in this book.

A Last Warning

We have seen the testimony of Jesus is the spirit of prophecy. If any man takes away the place of Jesus that God has given Him, the result is death.

Have you ever seen this happen? I have. I was raised in a church that was doing it. They took the place of Jesus away and didn't glorify Jesus. They didn't look to Jesus as the Head of the Church. Spiritual death was the result. Thank God that church has since been revived, but for a long, long time it was in spiritual death.

The Book of Revelation concludes with these inspiring verses:

REVELATION 22:20–21
20 He which testifieth these things saith, Surely I come quickly. Amen. Even so, come, Lord Jesus.
21 The grace of our Lord Jesus Christ be with you all. Amen.

Prayer of Salvation
to Receive Jesus as Savior

Dear Heavenly Father,

I come to You in the Name of Jesus.

Your Word says, *"The one who comes to Me I will by no means cast out"* (John 6:37 NKJV). I know You won't cast me out. You take me in, and I thank You for that.

You said in Your Word, *"Whoever calls on the name of the Lord shall be saved"* (Romans 10:13 NKJV). I am calling on Your Name, and I know You have saved me.

You also said, *"If you confess with your mouth the Lord Jesus and believe in your heart that God has raised Him from the dead, you will be saved. For with the heart one believes unto righteousness, and with the mouth confession is made unto salvation"* (Romans 10:9–10 NKJV). I believe in my heart Jesus Christ is the Son of God. I believe He died on the cross and was raised from the dead to pay the penalty for my sins. I confess Him as my Lord.

Because Your Word says that *"with the heart one believes unto righteousness,"*—and I do believe with my heart—I have now become the righteousness of God in Christ (2 Corinthians 5:21). I am now saved!

Thank You, Lord!

Signed ____

Date ____

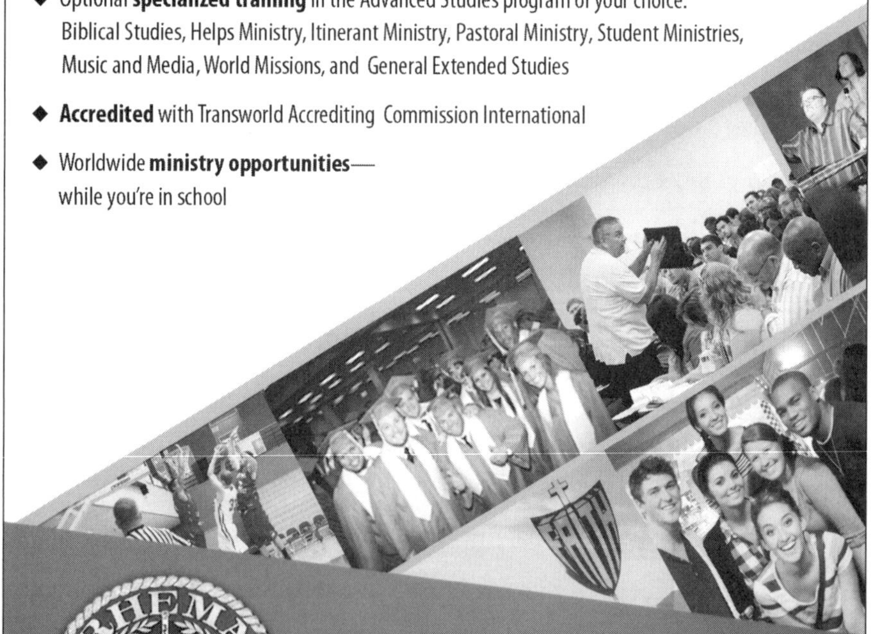